HoopMania:

THE BOOK OF BASKETBALL HISTORY AND TRIVIA

Brad Herzog

Sports Illustrated
KIDS
B O O K S

This Library Edition First Published and Exclusively Distributed by
The Rosen Publishing Group, Inc.
New York

To the top three sports heroes of my youth – Walter Payton, Michael Jordan, and Harold Baines. – B.H.

This library edition first published in 2003 and exclusively distributed by The Rosen Publishing Group, Inc., New York

Copyright © 2003 SPORTS ILLUSTRATED FOR KIDS Books

Book Design: Michelle Innes
Additional editorial material: Nel Yomtov

Photo credits: Cover (left), p. 124 © Icon Sports Media, (center), p. 113 © NBAE/GETTY IMAGES, (right), p. 138 © Duomo/CORBIS; backround and fast fact images © Picturequest; pp. 9, 22, 28, 39, 45, 52, 68, 73, 81, 93, 108, 117, 130 © Bettmann/CORBIS; p. 86 © Neal Preston/CORBIS; p. 103 © Naismith Memorial Basketball Hall of Fame

First Edition

Library of Congress Cataloging–in–Publication Data

Herzog, Brad.
  Hoopmania : the book of basketball history and trivia / Brad Herzog.—1st ed.
      v. cm.
"Sports illustrated for kids books"—T.p. verso. #8650258
Includes bibliographical references and index.
Contents: Basketball begins, 1500–1929 — When college was king, 1930–1945 — The start of the NBA, 1946–1959 — The age of Wilt, 1960s — Basketball rocks and rolls, 1970s — Magic time, 1980s — Basketball today, 1990s.
  ISBN 0–8239–3697–X (lib. bdg.)
 1. Basketball—United States—History—Juvenile literature. 2. Basketball—United States—Miscellanea—Juvenile literature. 3. Basketball players—United States—Anecdotes—Juvenile literature. [1. Basketball—History.] I. Title.
  GV885.1 .H467 2003
  796.323'0973—dc21

                        2001008744

>> CONTENTS

>> INTRODUCTION

Basketball celebrated its 100th anniversary in 1991 — and the game gets more exciting each season. Since its invention, basketball has gone through lots of changes, introduced us to many heroes, and provided buckets of magical moments.

HoopMania: The Book of Basketball History and Trivia takes you on a fun-filled flight through basketball history, from peach baskets to breakaway rims, from the first game to the last championship game.

The book is divided into eight sections. The first seven sections cover a different era of the game. In each part, you'll read about great games and superstars, and discover fascinating facts. The last section, Peak Performances, is a "Who's Who" statistical tribute to the NBA's greatest teams and League-Leading players.

Did you know that the score of the first public basketball game was 5–1? That men weren't allowed to watch the first women's college game? That the first Olympic gold–medal game was held outside, in the rain? That the dunk was once outlawed?

HoopMania tells these stories and many more, and introduces you to all of basketball's big names, from Dr. James Naismith to Doctor J, from George Mikan to Michael Jordan, from Maude Sherman to Cynthia Cooper. Read on to discover how the game of basketball has grown into the highest–flying sport of all!

>> BASKETBALL BEGINS

1500–1929

1500 HEADS UP!

Games using a ball and a hoop were played in Mexico hundreds of years ago. In the 1500s, the Aztec Indians played a game called *Ollamalitzli*. Ollamalitzli was a tough game. A player who made a shot was entitled to the clothing of all the spectators, and the captain of the losing team often had his head chopped off.

1891 THE GAME IS BORN

No one really invented baseball or football; they grew out of other games. But basketball, as we know it, is the invention of one man: Dr. James Naismith.

In 1891, Dr. Naismith was a physical education teacher at the YMCA Training School in Springfield, Massachusetts. (The school later became known as Springfield College.)

That autumn, the head of the physical education department noticed that the students were bored with the usual indoor exercise activities: calisthenics and gymnastics. He asked Dr. Naismith to come up with a new game the students could play.

Dr. Naismith tried to adapt outdoor sports, such as rugby, soccer, and lacrosse, to the gymnasium. However, each sport became too dangerous when it was played in a small indoor area. So in December, Dr. Naismith sat down to invent a new game using a round ball and a pair of goals.

BOXBALL?

If not for fate, Dr. Naismith's new game might have been called "boxball."

The game was tried for the first time by members of Dr. Naismith's gym class. Before the game, Dr. Naismith asked the school's janitor, Pop Stebbins, to find two boxes that could be used as goals. Pop could not find boxes, but he did come up with a pair of peach baskets. The baskets were nailed to the lower rail of the balcony in the school gym. The rail just happened to be 10 feet off the ground.

Those were two important developments in the history of basketball — and they both happened by accident. If Pop had been able to find what Dr. Naismith had asked for and if the gym balcony had been two feet higher, basketball players today might be shooting at boxes 12 feet off the ground.

Some people suggested that the game be called Naismith-ball, but Dr. Naismith preferred to call it "basket ball."

WEIRD RULES

The game Dr. Naismith invented was different from the game we know today. For one thing, there were nine players to a side (instead of five), because there were 18 students in Dr. Naismith's gym class. A field goal counted as only one point (instead of two), and a team could also earn a point if the opposing team committed three consecutive fouls. Players could not dribble, and there were no free throws or backboards. The ball could be moved only by passing and there were very few points scored.

BIG SHOT

William Chase is credited with scoring the first basket of the first basketball game. This took place during a scrimmage, or practice game, between members of Dr. Naismith's physical education class. William made history with a shot from 25 feet out — one foot three inches farther than an NBA three-point field goal. That first basket was also the only basket of the game.

LEGEND:

DR. JAMES NAISMITH

Dr. James Naismith, the inventor of basketball, originally planned to become a minister. He studied at McGill University in Montreal, Canada, where he competed in rugby, soccer, lacrosse, track, and tumbling. He was twice named the university's top all-around athlete.

Dr. Naismith decided that physical education was his favorite way to work with people, so he took a job as a physical education instructor in Springfield, Massachusetts. There, in late 1891, he invented basketball. The game spread across the country as his former students went on to start basketball programs at other colleges and YMCAs.

In 1895, at the age of 34, Dr. Naismith moved to Denver, Colorado. There, he attended Gross Medical School (now the University of Colorado School of Medicine) and received his medical degree. But the doctor still preferred to teach sports, and became the director of physical education at the University of Kansas. He coached the Kansas basketball team from 1899 to 1912 and remained an instructor at the school until he retired in 1937.

1892 THE FIRST OFFICIAL GAME

Basketball made its first public appearance on March 11, 1892. The students of Springfield College competed against their teachers in front of a crowd of about 200 people. The students won, 5–1.

WOMEN COME TO PLAY

Dr. Naismith was glad to see women take an interest in his game. The first women's basketball game took place in 1892 at the YMCA in Springfield. One of the players in that game, Maude Sherman, later married Dr. Naismith.

In 1893, Dr. Naismith explained the game to Senda Berensen, the director of physical education at Smith College, a women's college in nearby Northampton, Massachusetts. That same year, the first women's college game was played between the freshmen and sophomore classes at Smith.

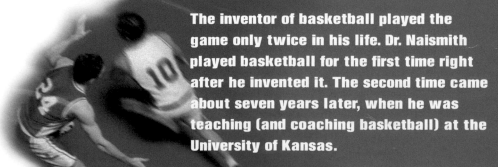

The inventor of basketball played the game only twice in his life. Dr. Naismith played basketball for the first time right after he invented it. The second time came about seven years later, when he was teaching (and coaching basketball) at the University of Kansas.

BUILDING A BETTER BALL AND BASKET

In its early years, basketball was played with a soccer ball. In 1894, a wheel manufacturer in Chicopee Falls, Massachusetts, made the first basketball by using tanned cowhide for the outside and a rubber bladder to hold the air on the inside. The ball had laces for gripping and looked like a round football.

The peach basket was soon replaced by a wire basket of the same shape. Like the peach basket, it was closed on the bottom. After a goal, someone had to use a long pole to poke the ball out of the basket or climb a ladder to lift the ball out.

In 1893, a company in Providence, Rhode Island, made a goal with an iron rim, a cord basket, and a pulley and chain so that after a goal was made the ball could be released by tipping the basket.

DESIGNATED SHOOTER

The idea of awarding a free throw to a team that had been fouled was introduced by Dr. Naismith in 1894. Up to that time, a team that had been fouled three times in a row was automatically given a point.

At first, all of a team's free throws were shot by the team's most accurate free-throw shooter. It wasn't until 1923 that a rule was added requiring free throws to be shot by the player who had been fouled.

Free throws were originally shot 20 feet from the basket. In 1895, the distance was shortened to 15 feet, where it stands today.

1895 THE FIRST MEN'S COLLEGE GAME

They never became a national power, but Hamline College of St. Paul, Minnesota, won the first men's college basketball game. Hamline defeated the Minnesota State School of Agriculture, 9–3, in 1895. There were nine players on each side. A year later, in the first college five-on-five game, the University of Chicago defeated the University of Iowa, 15–12.

FAMOUS AMOS

In 1892, Amos Alonzo Stagg played in the first official basketball game. The students played the teachers of Springfield College. Amos scored the only basket for the teachers. In 1896, as the first basketball coach at the University of Chicago, he coached in the first college five-on-five game. But basketball is not the sport Amos is most remembered for.

He is more famous for his role in developing the game of football. He won 314 football games as a college coach. He also invented the huddle, the reverse play, and the tackling dummy.

When he was 81, Amos was still coaching football, at the University of the Pacific, and was named Coach of the Year. He was the only person elected to the basketball and football halls of fame.

Amos retired at 98 and lived to be 103. He was born about the same time as Dr. Naismith, but he died the same year current NBA star Scottie Pippen was born!

Winning percentage is the number of games a team has won compared with the number of games it has played. The best single-season winning percentage by a National Basketball Association (NBA) team was achieved by the Chicago Bulls. The Bulls won 72 of the 82 games they played during the 1995–96 season, for an amazing .878 winning percentage.

Winning percentage is determined by dividing the number of games a team has won by the number of games it has played. For example, if a team wins five games and loses four, its winning percentage is five divided by nine, which is .555. If a team plays 82 games and wins 53, what is its winning percentage? You can find the solution by using the formula to the right. *(Check your answer on page 148.)*

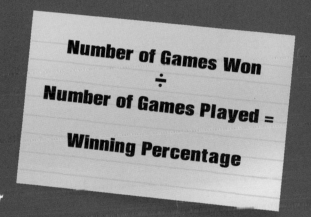

Number of Games Won

÷

Number of Games Played =

Winning Percentage

BASQUETTE: A GAME FOR LADIES

In many parts of the country, women's basketball developed into a different game from men's basketball. That started because of a mistake.

In 1895, Clara Baer, a physical education instructor in New Orleans, wrote to Dr. Naismith, requesting a copy of the rules of basketball. Dr. Naismith not only sent a

Only 13 NCAA Division I men's college basketball coaches have recorded at least 700 career victories. Dean Smith, the head coach at the University of North Carolina from 1962-97, recorded his 879th career victory in 1997. Entering the 2001-02 season, here are the members of the 700-win club.

Dean Smith (879)

* Jerry Tarkanian (759)

Adolph Rupp (876)

Phog Allen (746)

* Jim Phelan (816)

* Lou Henson (740)

Henry Iba (767)

Norm Stewart (731)

* Bob Knight (764)

Ray Meyer (724)

* Lefty Driesell (762)

Don Haskins (719)

Ed Diddle (759)   * Active

copy of the rules, he sent a diagram with lines on the court showing where players could be positioned. But Clara thought the diagram showed the areas players were not allowed to leave.

Clara's version of the game — which she called "Basquette" — became part of the first official women's basketball rules, which were set in 1899. They were quite different from the men's rules. The court was divided into three sections, and any player who left the section she was placed in was called for a personal foul. In addition, players weren't allowed to steal the ball from each other.

Later, the rules for this version of women's basketball were changed to have teams with six players to a side. For many years, girls and women continued to play six-person basketball. Three guards stayed at one end of the court for defense, while three forwards took shots at the other end. Nobody was allowed to cross the midcourt line.

Dribbling wasn't allowed in the early women's game, and even by the 1950s women were allowed to dribble the ball only twice before taking a shot.

BASKETBALL FREE-FOR-ALL

Basketball spread quickly after it was invented, moving to colleges and then to high schools. But there was no national set of rules until 1915. There was, however, a lot of confusion. Some teams played in basements that had nine-foot ceilings and floor-to-ceiling pillars right on the court. Some teams played with five players to a side, while others played with seven or more. In one exhibition played at Cornell University soon after basketball's invention, there were 100 players on the floor at the same time.

Because some schools were just learning the sport, several match–ups were quite uneven. In one game, Bucknell University defeated the Philadelphia College of Pharmacy, 159–5!

1896 THE FIRST PROS

The first known professional basketball game was played in 1896 in Trenton, New Jersey, by YMCA teams from Trenton and Brooklyn, New York. The Trenton team won, 16–1. When the gate receipts were split, each player earned $15.

The first pro league, the National Basketball League (NBL), was formed in 1898. It included six teams from the Philadelphia, Pennsylvania, area. The teams were Trenton, Camden, Millville, the Germantown Club, the Hancock Athletic Club, and the Pennsylvania Bicycle Club. The league lasted just five years.

THE FIRST PRO UNIFORMS

In the first professional basketball game, the competitors wore long tights and velvet shorts. It was far different from today's typical uniform. In fact, basketball was so rough around the turn of the century that players often dressed like football players. They wore heavy shirts and pants, and pads on their shins, knees, and elbows.

WHY CAGERS?

Basketball players are sometimes called "cagers." That term comes from the first few decades of basketball when the

In 1895, a group of 14-year-olds from a German neighborhood in Buffalo, New York, gathered at a local YMCA to form a basketball team. They were coached by Fred Burkhardt, who had learned the game from Dr. Naismith. They called themselves the Buffalo Germans.

The Germans were so good that in 1901, they won a game by a score of 134–0. That same year, they coasted to the national amateur championship. Three years later, they won the basketball tournament at the Olympic Games in St. Louis, Missouri, where basketball was a demonstration sport.

Over the years, the Germans played all sorts of teams, including college squads and YMCA teams. Older players were replaced by younger ones, but through it all the team kept winning. Beginning in 1908, they won 111 straight games over three seasons. The average score of those games was 54–18.

By the time the team broke up in 1929, the Germans had put together a record of 729 wins and only 86 losses. That's a winning percentage of .891. The entire original team was elected to the Basketball Hall of Fame.

In 1931, the original members of the Buffalo Germans got together for a game, 36 years after they had first played as a team. Even though they were each about 50 years old, they were still good enough to beat a team of younger men.

You are a freshman basketball player at Smith College, a women's college in Massachusetts, and you are nervous. After all, this isn't only your first basketball game, it's the first women's college basketball game ever.

It is March 22, 1893, and your freshman class has challenged the sophomores to a game. You have been practicing for three weeks, and it is finally time to play. At 8 P.M., each team of 12 players marches into the gym. Both teams are wearing heavy blue uniforms, including long-sleeve blouses and ankle-length skirts. As a member of the freshman team (Class of 1896), you have a purple number "96" stitched on the back of your uniform.

Nearly 300 women have filled the gym to watch, but there are no men. Men are banned from the area because it is not considered proper for them to see women playing basketball in their uniforms. The reporters covering the game are women, and the windows of the gym are covered.

The game begins. It is rough, and the players are aggressive. One player even dislocates her shoulder.

The game is 30 minutes long, with two 15 minute halves. When it is over, the sophomores have won, 5–4. You and your teammates present the winners with a white satin banner in honor of their victory. But the real victory is for all women and girls!

courts were often surrounded by wire, steel, or rope mesh.

One of the original rules of basketball stated that "when a ball goes out–of–bounds, it shall be thrown into the field by the first player touching [it]." That rule resulted in players diving into the stands and down stairways to be the first to touch a ball that had gone off the court. The "cages" were built to protect spectators and the players themselves.

UMBRELLA-TENDING

The backboard was introduced in 1896, but not to help shooters bank the ball into the basket. The real purpose of the first backboard was to keep spectators sitting behind the basket from interfering with shots. Fans would reach out from the stands, often with umbrellas, to swat away the opposing team's shots as they neared the basket.

HOW THE BALL BOUNCED . . .

Players on the Yale University team shocked the basketball world in 1896, when they became the first team to dribble the ball in competition. Rules were quickly introduced to restrict the practice. It wasn't until 1929 that all limitations on dribbling were eliminated and players were allowed to dribble as they do today.

. . . AND BOUNCED AND BOUNCED

Dutch Wohlfarth, a member of the Trenton YMCA team that played in the first pro game, was probably the first basketball star. Dutch could dribble the ball without

looking at it. He became famous — and drew crowds to Trenton's games — as "The Blind Dribbler."

LEAGUES OF THEIR OWN

The first college basketball leagues were formed in 1901. That year, Cornell, Columbia, Harvard, and Princeton formed the Eastern League, while Dartmouth, Amherst, Holy Cross, and Williams created the New England League.

THE FIRST FAST BREAK

A fast break is a basketball play in which the team with the ball races downcourt and tries to get off a good shot before the other team can get back into defensive position. The first team to use the fast break successfully was the Troy (New York) Trojans, known as Wachter's Wonders after star (and coach) Ed Wachter. In 1915, the Trojans won 29 games and lost none on a 39–day tour of the Midwest.

The Trojans are also credited with pioneering the bounce pass. The bounce pass is a pass delivered to a teammate on one bounce, usually to get the ball under a defensive player's outstretched hand.

A REALLY BIG SHOE

In 1917, the Converse Rubber Company, of Malden, Massachusetts, introduced its All–Star basketball shoe. Several years later, a former pro named Chuck Taylor

FAST BREAK

In the early days, basketball was often called "basket football," or "football in a gym." A half-period was called an "inning" and a goal was called a "touchdown."

was hired to drive around the country giving clinics and selling "Connies" out of the trunk of his Cadillac. In 1936, Converse added Chuck Taylor's name to the shoe. Through the years, the shoes have been known as "Cons" or "Chucks," and they are still popular today.

LONG-PLAYING RECORDS

From 1919 to 1925, the Passaic (New Jersey) High School boys' team set a high school record winning 159 consecutive games. From 1947 to 1953, the Baskin (Louisiana) High School girls' team did even better, winning 218 games in a row and seven straight state championships.

1928 THE LITTLE SCHOOL THAT COULD

In 1928, Carr Creek, a high school in Kentucky with only eight male students, nearly won the Kentucky state boys' basketball championship!

LEGEND:

NAT HOLMAN

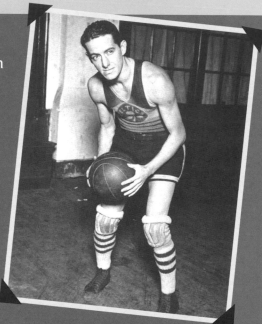

It is safe to say that no person in history saw more basketball than Nat Holman did. Nat was born in October 1896, just a few years after basketball was invented. He died on February 12, 1995, at age 98.

Nat was able to watch all the great teams in the history of the game — from the Buffalo Germans of the 1920s and the Boston Celtics of the 1960s to the Chicago Bulls of the 1990s. Nat also got to see all of basketball's best players — from George Mikan to Wilt Chamberlain to Michael Jordan.

But Nat also played on one of the game's best teams and coached another. In fact, before George, Wilt, Michael, and other stars were even born, Nat ranked as one of the best ever to play the game.

As a member of the Original Celtics in the 1920s, Nat became one of basketball's first great passers and dribblers. Largely because of Nat's skills, the Celtics were one of the most important and innovative teams ever to take the court. They showed the nation how creativity and teamwork could result in success (*see page 24*).

Nat was also a legendary coach. He coached the City College of New York (CCNY) men's basketball team for 42 seasons. In 1950, CCNY became the only team ever to win both the NCAA tournament and the National Invitation Tournament (NIT) in the same year. Nat was elected to the Basketball Hall of Fame in 1964.

The Creekers, who played their home games on an outdoor court carved out of a mountainside, made it all the way to the state finals. Fans all around the country were rooting for them. The final game went into four overtimes before the Creekers lost to Ashland.

WONDER FIVE

Long before the University of Michigan's Fab Five, there was St. John's University's Wonder Five. From 1927 to 1931, they were the best college team in the nation. The five stars — Mac Kinsbrunner, Allie Schuckman, Rip Gerson, Max Posnak, and Matty Begovich — played together from their freshman seasons on.

The team, coached by Buck Freeman, won 86 games over four seasons and only lost eight. After graduation, the five stars stayed together for five more seasons in the pro American Basketball League (ABL), where they called themselves the Brooklyn (later New York) Jewels.

In 1914, a group of talented basketball players formed a team called the New York Celtics. The team broke up during World War I, but a promoter named Jim Furey reorganized the squad after the war. Jim renamed his squad the Original Celtics, and they went on to become one of the most important teams in basketball history.

Jim recruited some of the nation's best basketball players for the Celtics, including Joe Lapchick, Dutch Dehnert, Nat Holman, and George "Horse" Haggerty. Until then, most professional players were paid per game and there wasn't any real team loyalty. But Jim signed his players for a full season, and his players gelled into an almost unstoppable squad.

The Celtics invented many of basketball's most basic concepts, such as post play (using the center as the hub of the offense), the give-and-go (when one player passes to another, then cuts to the basket to receive a return pass and make an easy score), and the zone defense (when a player guards whichever player comes into his area of the court, instead of covering a specific player man-to-man).

The Celtics scheduled more than 100 games a year and won most of them. They joined the American Basketball League in 1926 and won two straight league titles. The league decided to break up the Celtics before the 1928–29 season. It was just about the only way to stop them.

OVERTIME

You've read about the beginning of basketball.
Now jump into these tricky basketball teasers.
After you answer them, check your score on
page 146.

1 Basketball has had many great college coaches.
But few have been as great as University of North
Carolina head coach Dean Smith, who had 879 wins.
What freshman helped Coach Smith lead North
Carolina to the 1982 national championship?

2 In 1891, Dr. James Naismith invented basketball.
Twelve years earlier, in 1879, a man in New Jersey
invented the electric light. Can you name *this* inventor?

3 Basketball was a demonstration sport at the
1904 Olympics. What was the nickname of the
U.S. basketball team that won the gold medal
at the 1992 Summer Olympics?

4 Each player earned $15 in the first professional
basketball game, in 1896. At that rate, what would
a player's salary have been for an 82-game season?

>> WHEN COLLEGE WAS KING

1930–1945

1931 HOOP HEAVEN

In 1931, the United States was in the midst of the Great Depression. Millions of people were out of work and many of them were homeless. In New York City, Mayor Jimmy Walker wanted to use the growing popularity of college basketball to raise money to help people who had been hurt by the Great Depression.

The mayor asked sportswriter Ned Irish to put together a college basketball tripleheader in Madison Square Garden, the city's famous arena. Over 16,000 fans attended. Two years later, a Garden septupleheader — seven games, lasting all day — attracted 20,000 fans. Madison Square Garden soon became the capital of college basketball.

FREE-THROW KING

Professional basketball had a lot of show business in its early years. One of its showmen was Harold "Bunny" Levitt. Bunny was only 5 feet 4 inches tall, but when it came to shooting foul shots, he was a giant. For several years in the 1930s, Bunny toured with the Harlem Globetrotters (*see page 50*). At halftime at every game, Globetrotters owner Abe Saperstein would offer $1,000 to anybody who could out-shoot Bunny in 100 free-throw attempts. Over the years, about 400 people tried. The best anyone ever did was hit 86 free throws. The worst Bunny ever did was hit 96 out of 100.

THE FATHER OF BASKETBALL COACHES

Forrest C. "Phog" Allen learned basketball while playing for Dr. James Naismith at the University of Kansas. In 1906, he scored 26 points in one game, which was then a school record. After attending medical school, he became a basketball coach himself – one of the greatest of all time.

Allen became the coach at Kansas, succeeding his mentor, Dr. Naismith, in 1919. He coached at Kansas for 37 years. Along the way, Coach Allen helped start the National Collegiate Athletic Association (NCAA) tournament and he introduced basketball into the Olympics (he coached the United States to its first gold medal in 1936). His Kansas teams won 771 games, 24 conference titles, and a national championship. One of his last acts as Kansas coach was recruiting the great Wilt Chamberlain.

Before he retired, Dr. Naismith gave Coach Allen a self-portrait. On it, the doctor had written, "FROM THE FATHER OF BASKETBALL TO THE FATHER OF BASKETBALL COACHING."

LEGEND:

BABE DIDRIKSON ZAHARIAS

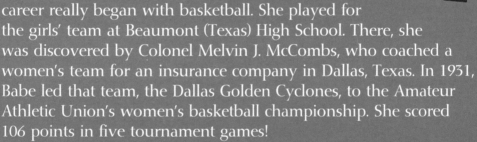

Babe Didrikson Zaharias may have been the best female athlete ever. She was born Mildred Ella Didrikson in Port Arthur, Texas, in 1914. She got her nickname at age seven after she hit five home runs in a baseball game with a group of boys. Babe Ruth was slugging home runs for the New York Yankees in those days, so the boys dubbed her "Babe."

Babe would make her mark in many sports. But her athletic career really began with basketball. She played for the girls' team at Beaumont (Texas) High School. There, she was discovered by Colonel Melvin J. McCombs, who coached a women's team for an insurance company in Dallas, Texas. In 1931, Babe led that team, the Dallas Golden Cyclones, to the Amateur Athletic Union's women's basketball championship. She scored 106 points in five tournament games!

Babe would go on to win two gold medals and a silver medal in track and field at the 1932 Summer Olympics. After the Olympics, she toured the country with her own basketball team. She also pitched in exhibition games for the Brooklyn Dodgers and St. Louis Cardinals, worked out with the Southern Methodist University football team, and toured the country playing billiards.

At the age of 20, Babe took up a new sport: golf. She was a founding member of the Ladies Professional Golf Association tour, and won 31 tournaments before she died of cancer in 1956, at age 42.

LOOK WORLD — ONE HAND!

On December 30, 1936, in New York City's Madison Square Garden, a great team met a great player. Long Island University was a basketball powerhouse. It had won 43 straight games coming into this game. But its opponent on that day, Stanford University (California), had Hank Luisetti, the first great one-handed shooter. More than 17,000 fans showed up for their first look at this West Coast wonder, and Hank didn't disappoint them.

Hank's first shot of the night was a one-hander over LIU's 6-foot-8 Art Hillhouse. *Swish*. Hank went on to score 15 points and lead Stanford to a 45–31 triumph over LIU. Long Island University's streak was over, but — thanks to Hank — an era of exciting basketball was just beginning.

1938 THE FIRST TOURNAMENTS

The first national college basketball tournament, the National Invitational Tournament, took place in 1938. It was introduced, in basketball-crazy New York City, by the local basketball writers' association.

That year, the sportswriters invited six of the best teams in the country to play in Madison Square Garden for the national championship. Those first six teams were New York University, Long Island University, Bradley University, Temple University, the University of Colorado, and Oklahoma A&M University (now Oklahoma State).

The first national title was won by Temple University, which beat Colorado in the NIT, 60–36. The star of the Colorado team was Byron "Whizzer" White, who was also the star of the Colorado football team and would later become a United States Supreme Court justice.

The NCAA started its own national championship tournament in 1939, selecting eight teams from different parts of the country. The first NCAA tournament was played in Evanston, Illinois. The champion was the University of Oregon, which defeated Ohio State in the final game, 46–33.

FAST BREAK

Until 1937, basketball had a rule that there had to be a jump ball between the two centers after every basket to decide which team got the ball on offense. You can imagine how that slowed the game down. The rule was changed to "losers' out" before the 1937–38 college basketball season. That means after a basket the ball goes to the team that was scored upon.

Scoring average measures how many points a player scores in a typical game. In the NBA, a scoring average over 20 is considered very good. The top single-season scoring average in NBA history is Wilt Chamberlain's average of 50.4 points per game for the 1961–62 season. The top career scoring average is Michael Jordan's 31.5 points per game.

A player's scoring average is figured by dividing the total number of points scored by the number of games played. Say a player scores 67 points in three games. His scoring average is 67 divided by three, or 22.3 points per game.

If a player plays in five games, and his per-game point totals are 24, 13, 15, 21, and 16, what is his scoring average? Use the formula to the right. *(Check your answer on page 148.)*

Total Points Scored
÷
Number of Games Played =
Scoring Average

Until the 1950s, the NIT was considered the more important tournament. Then the NCAA tournament passed it by and has grown more popular ever since. Today, the NIT still exists, but as two events: a pre–season tournament, and a post–season tournament for teams that are not invited to the NCAAs.

TELEVISION TUNES IN

Dr. James Naismith, the inventor of basketball, died at the age of 78 on November 28, 1939. Exactly three months later, a college basketball game was broadcast on television for the first time.

The telecast game was a match between Fordham University and the University of Pittsburgh at Madison Square Garden. It was seen on a few hundred television sets in New York City. (Most people did not own televisions at the time.) The broadcast was complete with technical problems, including a 20-minute blackout. The Fordham Rams won the historic contest, 57–37.

WONDER WOMEN

From 1915 to 1940, one team of women dominated almost every basketball court on which they played. The team was the Edmonton Commercial Grads. The Grads were all women who had graduated from Edmonton Commercial High School, in Alberta, Canada.

The Grads, who were mostly teachers and stenographers, went barnstorming through North America and Europe.

LEGEND:

HANK LUISETTI

Angelo "Hank" Luisetti played for the Stanford University (California) basketball team in the late 1930s. He was a great all-around player, but he became famous for introducing the one-handed shot.

Until Hank came along, the two basic shots in basketball were the layup and the two-handed set shot. Although Hank held the ball in both hands at the start of his shot, he released and guided the ball with the fingertips of one hand. It was like today's jump shot — without the jump.

As a kid growing up in San Francisco, Hank had to wear braces to correct his bowed legs. He developed his special shot because he was smaller than most of the kids with whom he played basketball. He had to step back to shoot over them, and he found that it was easier to reach the basket with a one-handed push shot.

The shot also enabled Hank to shoot the ball quicker than he could with two hands. That quickness, combined with his foot speed and dribbling ability (he also pioneered the behind-the-back dribble), made Hank look like a player from the future compared to the other players of his day.

The 6-foot-3 star averaged 20 points per game as a freshman at Stanford. By the time he graduated, he had scored 50 points in a game and 1,596 in his career. Both totals were NCAA records at the time. Hank never played in the NCAA tournament or as a professional. But in a few short years, he changed the game forever.

(A barnstorming team plays against local teams for a share of the money made from ticket sales.) The Grads won 522 out of 542 games, including 147 in a row. They beat men's squads seven of the nine times they played them.

HERE COMES THE JUMP SHOT!

When Kenny Sailors was growing up in Hillsdale, Wyoming, he often played basketball with his brother Bud. It wasn't an even matchup — Bud was eight inches taller than Kenny. Kenny needed a way to shoot the ball over Bud's outstretched hands. So, he began to jump before shooting. The jump shot was born.

Kenny went on to play basketball at the University of Wyoming. There he became the first player ever to use the jump shot in college competition. In 1943, the Wyoming team defeated Georgetown University for the NCAA title. Kenny was named Most Valuable Player of the tournament.

1944 SPLIT DECISION

In 1944, Melvin Stuessy coached two Illinois high school teams — St. Mary's and Hebron. At the end of the season, both teams competed in their district tournament. They played so well that they both reached the finals — where they had to face each other. St. Mary's won 33–30. A newspaper reported that "Coach Melvin Stuessy's Green Giants lost to Coach Melvin Stuessy's Fighting Saints." Talk about an up–and–down day.

THE 12,000-REBOUND CLUB

Only 16 players have grabbed at least 12,000 career rebounds. Entering the 2002-03 season, here are the men who have ruled the boards.

Wilt Chamberlain (23,924)

Bill Russell (21,620)

Kareem Abdul-Jabbar (17,440)

Elvin Hayes (16,279)

Moses Malone (16,212)

Robert Parish (14,715)

Nate Thurmond (14,464)

Walt Bellamy (14,241)

Wes Unseld (13,769)

* Hakeem Olajuwon (13,748)

* Karl Malone (13,973)

Buck Williams (13,017)

Jerry Lucas (12,942)

Bob Pettit (12,849)

Charles Barkley (12,546)

Paul Silas (12,357)   * Active

You are thousands of miles from home, and very few people here are familiar with your sport. You're a member of the United States men's basketball team that is competing in the 1936 Summer Olympic Games, in Berlin, Germany. This is the first time that basketball is an official Olympic sport.

You are expected to win the gold medal, but there are some obstacles in your way. The International Basketball Federation has voted to ban players who are 6 feet 3 inches or taller. The rule would prevent many of your teammates from playing. The Americans protest until the rule is changed.

But there's more. The games are played outdoors on old clay tennis courts. The clay surface makes you slip and slide when you try to change direction. The German-made basketballs wobble when they are thrown, and they are so light that the wind blows them around when you pass or shoot.

Still, your team makes it to the gold-medal game, where you will face the squad from Canada. The night before the big game, a rainstorm soaks the court. The swampy surface makes it almost impossible to dribble, but somehow your U.S. team is able to win, 19–8.

When it's all over, your uniform and shoes are covered with mud, but you have a gold medal around your neck and a smile on your face.

WHAT A FINISH!

The championship game of the 1944 NCAA tournament featured a team from the West, the University of Utah, against a team from the East, Dartmouth College. More than 15,000 fans were on hand for the game at Madison Square Garden.

The score was tied with three seconds left in the overtime period. That's when Utah's Herb Wilkinson took a shot from the top of the key. The ball hung on the rim for what seemed like forever, then fell through the basket. Utah had won its only national championship.

THE FIRST SEVEN-FOOTER?

The man known as basketball's first seven-footer was really only 6 feet 10 and one-quarter inches tall. He was Bob Kurland. Bob was an all-America center at Oklahoma A&M, and led the school to the NCAA title in 1945 and 1946. He was called a seven-footer because that attracted crowds to see him at A&M's games.

Bob had a habit of swatting opponent's shots off the rim. That led to the creation of the goaltending rule in 1945. The rule prevents players from interfering with a shot when the ball is on its way down toward the basket or when the ball is on or directly over the rim.

1945 A QUIET, 800-GAME WINNER

In 1945, 22–year–old Clarence "Big House" Gaines was hired as head basketball coach at Winston–Salem State College, in North Carolina. (Winston–Salem competes in Division II of the National Association of Intercollegiate Athletics, an organization similar to the NCAA.)

At his first coaching clinic, someone asked Coach Gaines if he was the janitor! Coach Gaines went on to become a legend. He won 800 games as a coach, making him one of only four coaches at a four–year college to pass the 800–win mark. The other coaches are Dean Smith of North Carolina, Adolph Rupp of Kentucky, and Jim Phelan of Mount St. Mary's in Maryland.

WORLD'S GREATEST DRIBBLER

Marques Haynes was a star with the Harlem Globetrotters (*see page 50*) and the Harlem Magicians for more than 40 years. Marques was known as "the world's greatest dribbler." He dribbled behind his back, through his legs, and while sliding on his side.

LEGEND:

GEORGE MIKAN

Believe it or not, for basketball's first 50 years, many observers believed that very tall people were too clumsy and slow to play the game. But George Mikan helped change all that.

George was not a great natural athlete. As a high school player in Joliet, Illinois, he was cut from his school team. In 1942, he enrolled as a 6-foot-10 freshman at Chicago's DePaul University to study law, not to play hoops.

But DePaul's coach, Ray Meyer, believed that George had great potential as a basketball player. Coach Meyer came up with drills that helped George develop his agility and basketball skills. By his sophomore year, George was ready to prove Coach Meyer right.

In those days, the three-second lane was just six feet wide, instead of 16 feet as it is today. When George positioned himself just outside the lane, he was almost unstoppable. He was a first team All-America in each of his final three collegiate seasons. In the semifinals of the 1945 NIT tournament, George scored 53 points — as many as the opposing team! George was named college Player of the Year as a junior and senior. The Associated Press honored him as the Player of the Half Century.

George played nine seasons of professional basketball, averaging more than 20 points per game as the NBA's first big star. He led the Minneapolis Lakers to five championships in six seasons.

It was a funny routine, but the first time he ever did it was in a real game. In 1945, Marques played college basketball for Langston University, in Langston, Oklahoma. Toward the end of a game between Langston and Southern University, Marques used his dribbling skills to protect Langston's lead. He dribbled around Southern players for two-and-a-half minutes, until time ran out.

Why did he choose that game to show off his dribbling routine? Marques was trying to get even with the Southern University team for embarrassing another conference school in a game played earlier in the season.

You've "passed" through some of the most
exciting basketball moments of the 1930s and
1940s. Now it's time to test your knowledge of
the game. If you need an "assist," the answers
are on page 146.

1 Georgetown University lost to jump-shooting Kenny
Sailors and his Wyoming teammates in the 1943 NCAA
championship game. What star NBA center led Georgetown
to its first national championship 41 years later?

2 Wilt Chamberlain has more rebounds (23,924) than any
player in basketball history. What outlandish former
NBA forward led the league in rebounds in seven straight
seasons from 1991-92 through 1997-98?

3 George Mikan was a star center with the Minneapolis
Lakers in the 1950s. Who starred at center for the Los
Angeles Lakers in the 1980s?

4 U.S. Supreme Court Justice Byron "Whizzer" White starred
for Colorado in the first NIT tournament. What former U.S.
Senator once starred in the NCAA tournament for Princeton?

>> THE START OF THE NBA

1946-1959

1949 NBL + BAA = NBA

There were plenty of attempts to form professional basketball leagues before the National Basketball Association (NBA) was formed in 1949. The NBA resulted from the merger of two earlier leagues — the National Basketball League (NBL) and the Basketball Association of America (BAA). The NBL had been formed in 1937, and the BAA had started in 1946.

WHAT'S A KNICKERBOCKER?

The Boston Celtics and the New York Knickerbockers (later shortened to Knicks) were two of the BAA teams. They are also the only teams from the original NBA that are still in the same city they started in.

The Boston Celtics were named for the Original Celtics, one of the great early pro basketball teams. The Knicks trace their nickname back to the early-American author Washington Irving.

In 1809, Washington Irving — using the pen name Diedrich Knickerbocker — wrote stories about the Dutch people who lived in New York City. After that, New Yorkers became known to many as "Knickerbockers."

BORN IN THE BAA

The Basketball Association of America was the birthplace of two important rule changes in professional basketball. The league's founders expanded the length of games from 40 minutes to 48 minutes. They also allowed players six personal fouls, instead of five, before they were disqualified.

OH, CANADA

The Toronto Huskies of the BAA were the first profes- sional basketball team located outside of the United States. Two Canadian teams joined the NBA in the 1995–96 season — the Toronto Raptors and the Vancouver Grizzlies. (The Grizzlies moved to Memphis, Tennessee in 2001.)

STICKING IT FROM HIS EAR

"Jumpin" Joe Fulks was the first pro player to perfect the jump shot. Joe's jumper was first called an "ear shot" because he launched it from next to his ear.

Joe sure could shoot. Playing for the Philadelphia Warriors (first of the BAA and later of the NBA), Joe once scored 63 points in a game against the Indianapolis Jets. For the 1946–47 season, Joe averaged a league–best 23.2 points per game while leading the Warriors to the BAA championship.

SCORING KINGS WHO WEAR CHAMPIONSHIP RINGS

Joe Fulks was one of only four men in NBA (and BAA) history to win both a scoring championship and a team championship in the same season. The other players were George Mikan, who did it in 1949 and 1950; Kareem Abdul-Jabbar, who led the NBA in scoring and carried the Milwaukee Bucks to a title in 1971; and Michael Jordan, who achieved both feats *six* times from 1991 through 1998!

THE ORIGINAL BACKBOARD BASHER

Long before Darryl Dawkins and Shaquille O'Neal shattered their first glass backboards, Boston Celtic Chuck Connors broke a *wooden* backboard. Chuck was a 6-foot-5 forward with the Celtics. He splintered the backboard in Boston Arena in 1946. It happened during the warm-ups before a BAA game against the Chicago Stags.

Chuck went on to become a well-known actor. He starred in *The Rifleman*, a television series that aired in the 1960s.

LEGEND:

ELGIN BAYLOR

Before Michael Jordan and Julius Erving took to the air, Elgin Baylor showed basketball players how to defy gravity. Elgin averaged 27.4 points and more than 13 rebounds per game during his 14–year career with the Minneapolis and Los Angeles Lakers. An 11–time All–Star, he scored 71 points in one game in 1960.

Elgin got his unusual name when his father glanced at his watch to check the time that his son was born. The first name his dad saw was Elgin, the name of the company that made the watch. As an African American growing up in Washington, D.C., Elgin did not start playing basketball until he was 14. Before that, the city's playgrounds were open only to white people.

Despite his Hall of Fame career, Elgin never won a championship. As a college player, he averaged 32.5 points a game for Seattle University in 1958, but his team lost to Kentucky in the final game of the NCAA tournament. As a pro, Elgin helped lead the Lakers to eight appearances in the NBA Finals, but they lost each time. Seven of those times were losses to the Boston Celtics.

Hobbled by injuries at the end of his career, Elgin retired nine games into the 1971–72 season. That season, the Lakers won the NBA title.

Assist average shows how many assists a player hands out in a typical game. In the NBA, an average of eight assists per game is very good. An average over 10 is excellent. John Stockton of the Utah Jazz averaged a record 14.5 assists per game during the 1989-90 season.

A player's assist average is figured by adding up the number of assists he has recorded and dividing that by the number of games he has played. For example, if he collects 27 assists in five games, his assist average is 27 divided by five, which is 5.4 assists per game.

Say a player plays in seven games, and his assist totals for those games are 8, 14, 7, 13, 12, 12, and 9. What is his assist average? To find out, use the formula to the right. *(Check your answer on page 148.)*

Total Assists
÷
Number of Games Played =
Assist Average

AUTHOR AND COACH

Clair Bee was a Hall of Fame coach and a successful author. As coach of the Long Island University Blackbirds, Clair had the best winning percentage (.827) in college history. While he was coaching, he began writing sports books for kids (he would write 23 in all) about a fictional high school athlete named Chip Hilton.

UH-OH

There is one basketball record that most record-holders aren't proud of. It is the record for the most field-goal attempts in a game without making one.

Howie Dallmar of the Philadelphia Warriors actually set it twice! He went zero for 15 in a 1947 game against the New York Knicks and he went zero for 15 again in a 1948 game against the Washington Capitols. But Tim Hardaway holds the record now. In 1991, he played for the Golden State Warriors and went zero for 17 in a game against the Minnesota Timberwolves. *Ouch.*

1950 TWO TITLES IN ONE SEASON

Today, the top 64 men's college teams are invited to the NCAA tournament, while the "next-best" 32 play in the National Invitation Tournament. However, in the early

FAST BREAK

Only one college basketball player has ever led the nation in scoring while also leading his team to an NCAA tournament championship. That player was Clyde Lovellette of the University of Kansas. Clyde, a 6-foot-9 forward, averaged 28.4 points per game during the 1951-52 season, and his Jayhawks breezed to the NCAA title.

days of college basketball's postseason tournaments, the best teams sometimes played in both. In 1950, City College of New York became the only school ever to win both tournaments in one year.

CCNY went 17–5 during the regular season. The school wasn't ranked among the nation's Top 20 and didn't have one All-America player. Yet, the CCNY Beavers made it to the NIT championship, where they rolled to a 69–61 upset victory over Bradley University (Illinois) at Madison Square Garden. Less than two weeks later, CCNY squeaked to a 71–68 win in the NCAA tournament final. That game was also played at Madison Square Garden, and Bradley was once again the losing team.

SCANDAL!

Less than a year after CCNY won both post-season tournaments, seven of the school's heroes were found to be villains. They were arrested for taking money from gamblers to fix games.

Eventually, an investigation revealed that 32 players from seven different colleges had fixed nearly 100 games over four seasons. They either lost games on purpose or made sure the final scores were closer than they should have been.

The scandal rocked college basketball. It was considered the darkest moment in sports since several members of the Chicago White Sox baseball team purposely lost the 1919 World Series.

LUCK OF THE CELTICS

In 1950, after the NBA's original franchise in Chicago folded, players from that team were divided among the other teams in the league. Finally, there were three players left and three teams for them to go to, but nobody wanted one of the players. He was a rookie guard named Bob Cousy.

The names of the three teams were put into a hat, and the "loser" — the Boston Celtics — had to take Bob. Some luck. Bob Cousy went on to lead the league in assists over eight straight seasons and help the Celtics win six NBA titles. He helped make the pro game popular with his great dribbling and exciting behind-the-back and no-look passes. Bob also averaged 18.4 points per game during his career and, in 1970, was elected to the Basketball Hall of Fame.

AFRICAN-AMERICAN PIONEERS

Until 1950, there were no African-American players in the major professional basketball leagues. That year, Charles Cooper, a second-round pick of the Boston Celtics, became the first black player drafted into the NBA. The first African American to play in a game was Earl Lloyd of the Washington Capitols. But perhaps the greatest pioneer of the NBA players was Nat "Sweetwater" Clifton. Nat was the first African American to sign with an NBA team, joining the New York Knicks in 1950.

He was a 6-foot-7 center and forward. In his first seven seasons in the NBA, Nat averaged 10.3 points and 8.5 rebounds per game.

Nat had to deal with spectators and teammates who criticized him because of the color of his skin or his style of play. He had played two seasons with the Harlem Globetrotters before joining the Knicks, and some people thought his moves on the court were too flashy for the NBA. But Nat ignored the insults and the criticism. He played hard, and eventually his style of play became an important part of the game.

Nat helped open the door for future black players. Because of him, men like Bill Russell, Julius Erving, and Earvin "Magic" Johnson were able to make their own important contributions to the game.

HARLEM GLOBETROTTERS

In 1951, a crowd of 75,000 people gathered in Berlin, West Germany (now Germany), to watch the Harlem Globetrotters play basketball. Only 15 years earlier, in 1936, German leaders had refused to honor African-American champions at the 1936 Summer Olympics in Berlin. But now the country was opening its arms to a group of black basketball wizards. That is what the Harlem Globetrotters are known for: making fancy passes and passing along good will.

The Globetrotters are a professional team that was started in 1927 by Abe Saperstein. Abe was small

Only 12 players in basketball history have scored at least 25,000 points in their careers. Entering the 2002-03 season, here's a list of the star players.

Kareem Abdul-Jabbar (38,387 points)

* Karl Malone (34,707 points)

Wilt Chamberlain (31,419 points)

* Michael Jordan (30,652 points)

Moses Malone (27,409 points)

Elvin Hayes (27,313 points)

Oscar Robertson (26,710 points)

Dominique Wilkins (26,668 points)

* Hakeem Olajuwon (26,946 points)

John Havlicek (26,395 points)

Alex English (25,613 points)

Jerry West (25,192 points)   * Active

(5 feet 3 inches), but he had big dreams. He organized an all-black team, gave them red-white-and-blue uniforms that he made in his father's tailor shop, and began to drive them around the country to play wherever they could.

LEGEND:

BILL RUSSELL

Bill Russell didn't make the varsity basketball team until his third year of high school, but he blossomed into a basketball legend.

In college, the 6–foot–9 center led the University of San Francisco to 55 consecutive wins and two national championships. After college, Bill led the U.S. basketball team to a gold medal at the 1956 Olympics. And in his 13 seasons with the Boston Celtics, the team won 11 NBA championships.

Bill helped to change the game by showing how a center playing intense defense could dominate the action. He averaged only 15.1 points per game throughout his career, but he grabbed an average of 22.5 rebounds per game.

The Celtic center was also an excellent shot–blocker. But he didn't just swat the ball out of bounds. He would grab the blocked shot in midair or tap it over to a teammate to start a fast break and get an easy basket.

Bill retired in 1969, but not before he changed the game in another important way. In 1966, he became player–coach of the Boston Celtics. That made him the first African American to coach a major professional sports team. As player–coach, he led the Celtics to the 1968 and 1969 NBA titles.

Soon Abe and the players realized that the best way for them to gain fans was to combine their basketball skills with a sense of humor. The Globetrotters began to spin the ball on their fingers, bounce the ball off their heads into the basket, line up like a football team — anything to amuse the crowd.

By 1950 the Globetrotters had traveled to Alaska, Mexico, Europe, Africa, and South America. They had truly become "globe-trotters." Still active today, they have performed in more than 100 countries around the world.

THE LONGEST GAMES

The longest game in NBA history was a game between the Indianapolis Olympians and the Rochester Royals on January 6, 1951. The game went to six overtimes and lasted nearly four hours. Indianapolis won, 75–73.

Thirty years later, the University of Cincinnati beat Bradley University in the longest major college basketball game in history. After seven overtimes, the final score was also 75–73.

There were 62 NCAA Division I men's championship games played from 1939 to 2001. But only five went into overtime. Perhaps the most exciting of those was a game played on March 23, 1957, between the University of North Carolina and the University of Kansas. That game went into triple overtime.

The North Carolina Tar Heels were 25–0 going into the game. The Kansas Jayhawks were led by 7-foot-1 superstar Wilt Chamberlain. The game was tied at the end of regulation time and at the end of two overtime periods.

With just seconds remaining in the third overtime, the Tar Heels clung to a 54–53 lead, but Wilt had the ball for the Jayhawks. He was almost unstoppable going to the basket, but this time he decided to pass. His pass was tipped away by Tar Heel Jack Quigg, who stole the ball. North Carolina held on and won its first national championship.

TWO-SPORT STARS

Dick Groat was a 6-foot guard from Duke University. He was one of the top players in the country during the 1950–51 basketball season. After playing one season of professional basketball, he switched to major league baseball. In 1960, as a shortstop with the Pittsburgh Pirates, Dick won the National League's Most Valuable Player Award.

Danny Ainge was a 6–foot–5 guard for Brigham Young University. In 1981, he won national college Player of the Year honors. However, Danny wanted to play professional baseball. He spent three summers (1978–80) with the Toronto Blue Jays and their minor league teams. Danny didn't become a baseball star (he batted only .220 as a big leaguer), so he turned to pro basketball. He helped the Boston Celtics win the NBA championship in 1984 and 1986.

1951 ALL STAR START

The first NBA All–Star Game was played in 1951. The league's Eastern Conference stars played its Western Conference stars. The team from the East won the first game, 111–94. Ed Macauley of the Boston Celtics was voted the Most Valuable Player.

Eleven years later, Wilt Chamberlain set an All–Star Game record by scoring 42 points. Kareem Abdul–Jabbar holds the All–Star Game records for most appearances (18) and most career points (251).

1952 A REAL ROAD GAME

Charlotte High School in Punta Gorda, Florida, didn't have its own gym. So the team played all its 1952–53 games on the road — except for one. The school's one home game, however, was actually played *on* a road. A basketball court was set up on Marion Avenue, the town's main street.

WHEN THE RIM WAS RAISED

Have you ever wondered what would happen if the baskets were raised from 10 feet to 12 feet? In a 1954 game between the Milwaukee Hawks and the Minneapolis Lakers, the NBA tried that bold experiment. The Lakers won, 65–63. But the teams made only 48 of 159 shot attempts. George Mikan, the Lakers' 6–foot–10 star, missed his first 12 shots.

HITTING FOR 100

The most points scored in a college game against a four-year school was 113. Clarence "Bevo" Francis of Rio Grande College (Ohio) set the record in 1954, against Hillsdale (Missouri) College in 1954. Bevo had scored 116 points against Ashland (Kentucky) Junior College, a two-year school, a year earlier.

The first player from a major college to score 100 points in a game was Frank Selvy of Furman College, in Greenville, South Carolina. Frank scored 100 points in a 1954 game against Newberry College. Frank's team won, 149–95.

A TIMELY IDEA

Danny Biasone is not a famous name in basketball, but he helped make the NBA famous. In the league's early days, teams often held the ball for long periods of the game if they were ahead. This made for low–scoring, boring games. In 1950, for example, the Fort Wayne

The Los Angeles Lakers are one of the most successful teams in the NBA. But before the Lakers moved to L.A. in 1960, they played in Minneapolis, Minnesota. The Lakers were pretty good there, too.

The Minneapolis Lakers were led by 6-foot-10 superstar George Mikan. The team's other leader was a foot shorter than George. He was 5-foot-10 guard Slater Martin. Together, they made the Lakers into the NBA's first dynasty.

The Lakers won three titles in a row — in three different pro basketball leagues. They won the National Basketball League title in 1948. The following season, they won the Basketball Association of America championship. The Lakers won the first NBA title in 1950. They won three more NBA crowns in 1952, 1953, and 1954. The only other teams to win three straight championships were the Boston Celtics of the 1960s and the Chicago Bulls of the 1990s.

Pistons defeated the Minneapolis Lakers, 19–18. The Pistons stalled for much of the game.

Danny owned the NBA's Syracuse Nationals. In 1954, he came up with the idea of the 24–second shot clock. Under his plan, a team had to shoot within 24 seconds after receiving the ball on offense.

Why 24 seconds? Danny reasoned that, in an exciting game, two teams should combine to take 120 shots. He figured out that there were 2,880 seconds in a 48–minute game. Then he divided 120 shots into 2,880 seconds. The answer was 24.

1957 WHAT A FINISH!

The Boston Celtics won nine NBA titles in 10 seasons between 1956 and 1966. But the Celtics had a close call in 1957.

Boston was playing the St. Louis Hawks in a championship series that had gone the full seven games. With time running out at the end of regulation play, Hawk star Bob Pettit sank two free throws to tie the game and send it into overtime. The game was still tied at the end of one extra period, so the teams played a second overtime.

FAST BREAK

Bud Grant was a reserve player for the NBA champion Minneapolis Lakers in 1950. He averaged 2.6 points per game in two seasons of professional basketball. But Bud went on to become one of the most famous sports figures in Minnesota history. As head coach of the National Football League's Minnesota Vikings, he led the team to four Super Bowl appearances in the 1970s.

You are a member of one of the world's best basketball teams, but you still can't find a hotel that will let you spend the night. You have entertained about 15,000 fans with your basketball skills, but you have trouble finding a restaurant that will serve you. You are one of the New York Renaissance Five, an all-black team. And because you are traveling the country at a time of widespread bigotry, you often have more trouble with fans than with opposing teams.

Your team is nicknamed the Harlem Rens because your home court is the second-floor ballroom of Harlem's Renaissance Casino in New York City. The team, founded by Bob Douglas in 1922, spends its time barnstorming the country. That means you travel from town to town, playing games against local teams and receiving a percentage of the money earned through ticket sales.

To make ends meet, you sometimes play as many as three games in one day. With players like 6-foot-5 "Wee" Willie Smith, 6-foot-4 Charles "Tarzan" Cooper, and 5-foot-7 Clarence "Fat" Jenkins, your team wins 473 of 522 games between 1932 and 1936. By the time the team disbands in 1949, it has won 2,588 games and lost only 529.

Eventually, you and your Harlem Rens teammates receive the respect you deserve. In 1963, you are inducted into the Basketball Hall of Fame.

Boston took a 125–123 lead on a free throw by Celtic forward Jim Loscutoff, with two seconds left in the second overtime. Then, Bob Pettit's last–second shot to tie the game bounced off the rim as time ran out. Boston had squeaked by with another NBA title.

A NAME TO KNOW

Who was the first great star of women's basketball? Babe Didrikson was amazing, but she had only a brief career in basketball before moving on to other sports. For sheer longevity, how about Nera White?

From 1955 to 1969, Nera led her Nashville Business College team to 10 Amateur Athletic Union (AAU) championships and was named MVP of the AAU tournament 10 times.

FAST BREAK

One of the Harlem Globetrotters' most popular acts involved the team's best jumper, Jimmy Jackson. The Globetrotters would place a quarter on top of the backboard, nearly 12 feet off the ground. Then Jimmy would jump up and come down holding the quarter.

In 1957–58, she led the United States women's national team to the World Championship and was again named MVP. Now that's a true star.

A WINNING COACH

Arnold "Red" Auerbach has been around even longer than the NBA. He started in the Basketball Association of America's first season, 1946, as the coach of the Washington Capitols. In 1950, he became the head coach of the Boston Celtics. Today, Red is the Celtics' vice-chairman of the board and president, but he is best remembered as one of the most successful coaches in NBA history.

Red's teams won a whopping 1,037 games. He won 938 regular-season games, 99 playoff games, and nine NBA titles. His Celtic teams won one title in 1957 and eight straight titles from 1959 through 1966. Talk about a winning streak.

Since Red first became associated with the Celtics in 1950, they have been one of the most successful teams in sports history. They have won 16 NBA titles, more than any other team. Red has coached and drafted some of the greatest players in league history, including Bob Cousy, Bill Russell, John Havlicek, and Larry Bird. No wonder the league's Coach of the Year trophy is named after him.

GO NON-SKIDS!

Many teams that were in the National Basketball League, the American Basketball Association, and the early NBA are no longer around. But they left behind some interesting nicknames. Some of those teams, like the Non-Skids (a brand of tire), were named after people or after products that the owners sold. These are some of the stranger team names basketball has seen:

San Diego Sails
Detroit Gems
Toledo Jeeps
Memphis Sounds
St. Louis Bombers
Minnesota Muskies
Kentucky Colonels
Fort Wayne General Electrics
Indianapolis Kautskys
Pittsburgh Ironmen
Oakland Oaks
Akron Firestone Non-Skids
Columbus Athletic Supply
Chicago Zephyrs

It's time for you to go one-on-one with these four trivia questions. The information in this book is sure to help you score. Check your answers on page 146.

1 In 1950, African Americans first began to play in the NBA. Then, in 1966, Bill Russell of the Boston Celtics became the first African American to coach a major professional sports team. What former Los Angeles Raiders coach was the first African-American head coach in the National Football League?

2 Jerry West is a member of the 25,000-point club. What NBA team did he play for?

3 The 24-second shot clock was introduced in the NBA in 1954. Men's *college* basketball uses a 35-second clock in games that are 40 minutes long. If each team shot every 35 seconds, how many shots would be taken in a regulation game?

4 The St. Louis Hawks won the 1958 NBA title. What city do the Hawks now call home?

>> THE AGE OF WILT

1960s

STRANGE NICKNAMES

There are no lakes in Los Angeles and not much jazz in Utah. The Los Angeles Lakers and the Utah Jazz got their nicknames from their original hometowns: Minneapolis (Minnesota) and New Orleans (Louisiana). Minnesota has about 20,000 lakes and New Orleans is considered the birthplace of jazz. The Lakers moved to L.A. at the start of the 1960–61 season and the Jazz played in Utah starting in 1979–80.

1960 HOT HEATER

On January 26, 1960, a high school player named Danny Heater set a national record by scoring 135 points in one game for Burnsville High School in West Virginia. Danny hit 53 of 70 shots and sank 29 of 41 free throws, an amazing total for a 32–minute game.

THE TREY IS BORN

The three–point shot didn't begin with the American Basketball Association (*see page 78*). It started with the

American Basketball League. The ABL was started by Abe Saperstein, founder of the Harlem Globetrotters, in 1961–62. The league lasted just 18 months, but it introduced the idea of awarding a team three points for making an especially long shot. In the ABL, three–point territory was 25 feet or more from the basket.

THE BIGGEST BIG MAN

The tallest person ever to play basketball is believed to be a man named Suleiman Ali Nashnush, who played for the national team of Libya, a country in northern Africa, in 1962. He was 8 feet tall, nearly a whole foot taller than Shaquille O'Neal.

THE MAGIC 100

Wilt Chamberlain's amazing 1961–62 season included three 62–point games in one eight-game stretch. That season, he also scored 65, 67 (twice), 73, and 78 points in a game. But March 2, 1962, was the day Wilt put on a performance that may never be matched. He set an NBA record by scoring 100 points in a game.

Wilt and the Philadelphia Warriors were playing the New York Knicks in Hershey, Pennsylvania. Wilt had 23 points in the first quarter and 41 by halftime. Four Knick players took turns trying to guard the big man.

At one point during the first quarter Knick center Darrell Imhoff was called for fouling Wilt. Darrell turned to one of the referees and said, "Why don't you just give him 100 points and we'll go home!"

Darrell sounded like a prophet, but no one was giving Wilt anything. He was unstoppable. With seven minutes and fifty-one seconds left, he scored his 79th point of the game. That broke the record for most points in an NBA game which Wilt had set three months earlier.

Wilt's teammates kept passing to him, and he kept scoring. The Warriors and most of the spectators wanted him to score 100. With about one minute remaining, Wilt had 98 points. Then, with 46 seconds left, he sank a shot to reach the magic 100!

The Warriors won, 169–147. Among the records Wilt set that day were marks for most field-goal attempts (63) and

FAST BREAK

Wilt Chamberlain of the Philadelphia Warriors averaged 50.4 points and 25.7 rebounds per game for the 1961–62 season — but he wasn't the NBA's Most Valuable Player. The players themselves voted on the MVP award, and they chose Boston Celtic center Bill Russell. Bill, who led the Celtics to the NBA title that season, was considered the greatest defensive player in the game. And the voters decided that Bill's defense was more important to his team than Wilt's offense was to his.

field goals made (36) in a game. He also set a record by hitting 28 of 32 free throws, even though he was usually a bad free-throw shooter. When you're hot, you're hot.

1962 IT'S ALL IN THE WRIST

Tommy Boyer of the University of Arkansas won the NCAA free-throw shooting title in 1962 with a single-season percentage of .933, setting an NCAA record. (Craig Collins of Penn State set the current record of .959 in 1985.) What made Tommy's achievement more amazing is that he was blind in one eye.

NO FOUL

Including regular-season, playoff, and All-Star games, Wilt Chamberlain played in 1,218 games in his 14-year NBA career. Wilt appeared on the court for 47,859 minutes, yet he never once fouled out. On the other hand, Vern Mikkelsen played in 790 games from 1949 to 1959 and fouled out a record 127 times.

20-20 VISION

Only four men in NBA history have averaged at least 20 points and 20 rebounds in the same season. Hall of Famer Bob Pettit, a forward for the St. Louis Hawks, averaged 27.9 points and 20.3 rebounds during the 1960–61 season. Jerry Lucas, a forward for the Cincinnati Royals did it twice. He averaged 21.4 points and

LEGEND:

WILT CHAMBERLAIN

When Wilt Chamberlain was just in high school, he was probably already the most dominant basketball player in the country. At 7 feet tall, Wilt was such a powerful player that more than 100 colleges recruited him when he graduated from Overbrook High School in Philadelphia, Pennsylvania. Wilt chose Kansas University, and he led the school to the finals of the NCAA tournament in his first season (1956–57).

By the time Wilt began his NBA career, in 1959, he was 7 feet 1 inch and almost 300 pounds. Some fans called him "Wilt the Stilt," but he preferred the nickname "The Dipper" (like the constellation, the Big Dipper). He led the league in scoring for seven straight seasons, a feat matched only by Michael Jordan. For his career, Wilt averaged 30.1 points and a record 22.9 rebounds per game. He holds the top four single-season scoring marks in NBA history.

When Wilt left basketball, he held or shared 43 records. He was the center of two teams with two of the best regular season records in NBA history: the 1966–67 Philadelphia 76ers (68–13) and the 1971–72 Los Angeles Lakers (69–13, with a record 33 wins in a row). Those were also his only two NBA championship teams. Seven times in Wilt's career his teams were beaten by Bill Russell's Celtics in the playoffs.

For all of his great skills, Wilt was never very popular with the fans. Perhaps that was because he was so big. "Nobody roots for Goliath," he once said.

20 rebounds in the 1964–65 season. Then he averaged 21.5 points and 21.1 rebounds in the 1965–66 season. Nate Thurmond, a forward with the San Francisco Warriors, averaged 20.5 points and 22 rebounds in the 1967–68 season. Wilt Chamberlain averaged at least 20 points and 20 rebounds per game from 1959 to 1969.

LEAGUE LEADER

Over 11 seasons, Bill Sharman was named Coach of the Year in three different leagues. In 1962, Bill coached the Cleveland Pipers to the championship of a new professional league — the American Basketball League. The league lasted just one season.

Almost 10 years later, Bill coached the Utah Stars to the championship of the American Basketball Association. The next season, Bill was hired by the NBA's Los Angeles Lakers. He led the Lakers to 69 victories and the 1972 NBA title.

The University of Cincinnati (Ohio) had won two straight national titles heading into the finals of the 1963 NCAA tournament. But the Bearcats' opponent in the championship game was the surprise team of the tournament — the Loyola University Ramblers from Chicago, Illinois. Midway through the second half, Cincinnati seemed to have a comfortable 45–30 lead, but Loyola came rambling back.

With just seconds left, the Bearcats led 54–52. Then Loyola's Jerry Harkness grabbed a rebound off a missed foul shot that would have given Cincinnati a three-point lead. He drove the length of the floor to tie the score and send the game into overtime.

In the extra period, the game went back and forth. Then, with 2:15 left to play, Loyola decided to hold the ball and try for the last shot (this was before the introduction of the 30-second clock in college basketball). With just four seconds to play, Loyola's Vic Rouse rebounded a missed shot and scored to give the Ramblers a 60–58 upset victory. The Cinderella team was champion.

ONE FROM THE PLAYGROUNDS

Here's one that may be more fable than fact. In 1963, Earl "Goat" Manigault, a legendary schoolyard player from Harlem in New York City, made one of basketball's most amazing dunks. Goat, who was just 6 feet 2 inches and was being guarded by two much taller college stars, took off at the foul line. He made two corkscrew revolutions before slamming the ball through the rim — or so the story goes.

LITTLE BEARS

The University of California at Los Angeles (UCLA) Bruins won the NCAA title in 1964 with no player taller than 6 feet 5 inches. The Bruins, coached by John Wooden, went 30–0 for the season. The title was the first of 10 that UCLA would win over the next 12 seasons.

1966 A DEFEAT FOR RACISM

University of Kentucky coach Adolph Rupp was one of the most successful college basketball coaches ever, winning a record 876 games in his career. But he was also a man known for his racial prejudices: He did not allow any African-American players on his team.

In 1966, Kentucky reached the title game of the NCAA tournament, where they ran into a team from Texas Western University (now known as Texas–El Paso). The team from Texas Western had an all–black starting five.

All five players were All–Americas.
The Texas Western Miners beat Adolph
Rupp's Wildcats, 72–65, to take the
national title.

NO DUNKING!

It's unbelievable, but true. In 1967,
the dunk was banned in high school
and college basketball. The rule-makers
claimed the dunk was outlawed to
prevent injury and equipment damage,
but many people believed it was to slow
down 7–foot–2 Lew Alcindor (Kareem
Abdul–Jabbar). The dunk was legalized
again nine years later.

THE TRIPLE-DOUBLE

Baseball has the Triple Crown (when a
player leads the league in batting average,
home runs, and runs batted in), and
basketball has the triple–double. A player
is credited with a triple–double when he
records double figures (10 or more) in a
game in three different statistical categories,
such as points, rebounds, and assists.

LEGEND:

OSCAR ROBERTSON

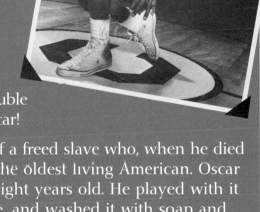

Oscar Robertson was the NBA's first great all–around player. He was a 6–foot–5 guard who played in the NBA from 1960–74. The "Big O" was a scorer, playmaker, and rebounder. He played in 12 All–Star Games and earned the Most Valuable Player Award in 1964.

For his career, Oscar averaged 25.7 points, 7.5 rebounds, and 9.5 assists per game. In fact, over his first five seasons, he averaged 30.3 points, 10.4 rebounds, and 10.6 assists per game. A triple–double was just an average night for Oscar!

Oscar was the great–grandson of a freed slave who, when he died at age 116, was believed to be the oldest living American. Oscar got his first ball when he was eight years old. He played with it on the dirt court near his home, and washed it with soap and water every night.

Oscar spent most of his NBA career with a team then known as the Cincinnati Royals (now the Sacramento Kings). But he never played on an NBA championship team until he was traded to the Milwaukee Bucks in 1970.

When Oscar joined the Bucks, he had his uniform number changed from 14 to number 1. "The only thing that matters in this game is being number one," he explained, "and we're aiming straight at it."

In the 1971–72 season, the "Big O" teamed with Lew Alcindor (later known as Kareem Abdul–Jabbar) to give the Bucks the NBA title.

Free-throw percentage measures how many free throws a player makes compared to how many free throws he attempts. In the NBA, a free-throw percentage over .800 is good. A percentage over .900 is great. The player with the best single-season free-throw percentage in NBA history is Calvin Murphy of the Houston Rockets, with a .958 percentage for the 1980-81 season.

Free-throw percentage is figured by dividing the number of free throws made by the number of free throws attempted. For example, if a player takes 20 foul shots and makes 16 of them, his free-throw percentage is equal to 16 divided by 20, or .800.

If a player attempts 66 foul shots and is able to sink 44 of them, what is his free-throw percentage? To find out, use the formula below. *(Check your answer on page 148).*

Free Throws Made

÷

Free Throws Attempted =

Free-Throw Percentage

FAST BREAK

Charles Biles coached a girls' basketball team at Red Boiling Springs High School, in Red Boiling Springs, Tennessee, during the 1964–65 season. At the same time, his wife, Freda, coached the Macon County High School girls' team in Lafayette, just 13 miles away. The teams met twice during the season, and Freda's squad won both times.

The triple-double wasn't kept as a statistic until 1980, when Earvin "Magic" Johnson began performing the feat regularly. Magic holds the record for the most triple-doubles, doing it 138 times in his career. During the 1981–82 season alone, he did it 18 times.

Oscar Robertson played before the triple-double stat was kept, but he *averaged* a triple-double for the 1961–62 season: 30.8 points, 12.5 rebounds, and 11.4 assists!

THE QUADRUPLE-DOUBLE CLUB

The triple-double is a great feat, but how about a quadruple-double? Only four men in NBA history have accomplished that since the stats were kept.

The Boston Celtics of the 1950s and 1960s were one of the greatest teams in sports history. From 1957 to 1969, Boston won 11 titles in 13 seasons, including an NBA-record eight straight championships from 1959–66.

The team was led by playmaking guard Bob Cousy (until he retired in 1963), shot-blocking center Bill Russell, and legendary coach Red Auerbach. But the Celtics continued to win long after their "golden years." Boston took two more titles in the 1970s (1974 and 1976), led by Dave Cowens, Jo Jo White, and John Havlicek. And the Celtics won three more championships in the 1980s (1981, 1984, and 1986), thanks to stars like Larry Bird, Robert Parish, and Kevin McHale.

In all, the Celtics have won 16 NBA championships. That's an average of one title every three years! The only teams that have come close to Boston's basketball success are Major League Baseball's New York Yankees and the National Hockey League's Montreal Canadiens.

Nate Thurmond of the Chicago Bulls was the first. On October 18, 1974, he collected 22 points, 14 rebounds, 13 assists, and 12 blocked shots. Nobody else did it for another 12 years, until February 18, 1986, when Alvin Robertson of the San Antonio Spurs had 20 points, 11 rebounds, 10 assists, and 10 steals.

The third person to record a quadruple–double was Hakeem Olajuwon, on March 29, 1990. The Houston Rockets center had 18 points, 16 rebounds, 11 blocks, and 10 assists. Finally, on February 17, 1994, David Robinson of the Spurs recorded 34 points, 10 rebounds, 10 assists, and 10 blocks.

1967 WILT, THE PLAYMAKER

Sometimes it seemed as if Wilt Chamberlain could succeed at whatever he did on a basketball court. He led the NBA in scoring seven times, and in rebounding average 11 times. During the 1967–68 season, Wilt decided to concentrate on passing the ball. He led the league with 8.6 assists per game, setting a record for centers.

WILTING ON THE LINE

For all his talents, Wilt Chamberlain could not shoot free throws very well. He was a .511 percentage shooter for his career. During the 1967–68 season, Wilt tried shooting free throws underhand. It did not help. He connected on just 38 percent of his free throw attempts that season.

THE ABA

In 1967, a new professional basketball league gave the NBA some competition. It was called the American Basketball Association, and it featured, among other things, a red, white, and blue basketball. The league also made use of the three-point shot, more than a decade before the NBA did, and hosted the first All-Star Game slam-dunk contest.

The ABA's first commissioner was George Mikan, the biggest star of the early days of the NBA. The Oakland Oaks beat the Anaheim Amigos 134–129 in the league's first game and the Pittsburgh Pipers won the first ABA title.

The ABA lasted just nine years and folded in 1976, but it gave basketball the three-point shot, the slam-dunk contest, and four of its teams — the Pacers, Spurs, Nuggets, and Nets. In 1976, all four joined the NBA.

THE FLIGHT OF THE HAWK

Connie Hawkins was the first player to lead a pro league in scoring despite having very little college experience. He dropped out of the University of Iowa in his freshman year because of a rumor that he had talked to gamblers about fixing games. The rumor was later proven false, but it kept Connie out of big-time basketball for what probably would have been his best years.

In 1962, Connie was MVP of the short-lived American Basketball League. From 1964–66, he played for the

A total of 52,693 fans witnessed a game between the University of Houston and the University of California at Los Angeles, on January 20, 1968, at the Houston Astrodome. At the time, it was the largest crowd ever to see a college basketball game. Houston was led by Elvin Hayes, whose nickname was "The Big E." UCLA, led by Lew Alcindor (Kareem Abdul-Jabbar), went into the game with a 47-game winning streak.

Elvin Hayes put on an amazing show, scoring 29 points in the first half, as Houston led 46–43. But the game grew even closer. It was tied at 54–54, 65–65 and finally at 69–69. With less than 30 seconds remaining, Elvin drove toward the basket and was fouled. He calmly sank both free throws to give Houston a two-point victory over the best team in college basketball. Elvin finished with 39 points and held Lew to just 15 points. The Big E also grabbed 15 rebounds.

The teams would meet again that season in the semi-final round of the NCAA tournament Final Four. This time Lew held Elvin to 10 points and the Bruins defeated the Cougars, 101-69, on their way to a second straight NCAA title.

Harlem Globetrotters. He joined the ABA in its first season, 1967–68, where he led the league in scoring, won the MVP award, and carried the Pittsburgh Pipers to a championship.

Connie later played seven seasons in the NBA — with the Lakers, Suns, and Hawks. In 1992, he was elected to the Basketball Hall of Fame.

1968 HALL CALL

The Naismith Memorial Basketball Hall of Fame opened on February 18, 1968, in basketball's birthplace, Springfield, Massachusetts. The Hall of Fame honors players, coaches, referees, and contributors from every level of the sport. James Naismith, Hank Luisetti, and George Mikan were among the first group elected to the shrine. As of 2001, 241 people and four teams have been enshrined in the Hall.

1969 REPEAT AFTER ME

The Boston Celtics won the NBA championships in 1967–68 and 1968–69. It took 18 seasons for another team to win back-to-back titles. Finally, in 1986–87

LEGEND:

BILL BRADLEY

Many kids dream of becoming a professional basketball player. Others dream of becoming President of the United States. Bill Bradley may be the first to do both.

Bill was not a great athlete, but he was dedicated to improving his game. As a boy, he would put lead in his sneakers to strengthen his legs, wear blinders to work on dribbling, and have his mother hold up a broom to help him practice shooting over defenses.

Bill was an All–America at Princeton University in the 1960s. He was captain of the 1964 U.S. Olympic basketball team. He led the team to a gold medal.

He was named college Player of the Year in 1965, when he led Princeton to the Final Four of the NCAA Tournament. After his team lost in the semifinals, Bill led Princeton to a third–place finish with a win in the consolation game. (The game for third place is no longer played.)

Bill took two seasons off from basketball after he graduated so that he could study at Oxford University in England as a Rhodes Scholar. When he returned, he joined the NBA's New York Knicks. In the pros, Bill was known for moving without the ball and playing tough defense. In his 10 pro seasons, he helped the Knicks win two NBA championships.

Soon after he retired, Bill entered politics. He was elected as a Senator from New Jersey and served for 12 years. Bill then ran for president in 2000, losing the Democratic Party nomination to Al Gore.

and 1987–88, the Los Angeles Lakers performed the feat. Repeating then became the rule, rather than the exception. The Detroit Pistons won in 1988–89 and 1989–90. The Chicago Bulls were champs in 1990–91, 1991–92, and 1992–93. The Houston Rockets broke the Bulls' string with titles in 1993–94 and 1994–95. But the Bulls stormed back in 1995–96, 1996–97, and 1997–98.

SWEET 16

In 1969, two Tennessee high schools — Voltewah and Chattanooga East Ridge — met and set a record that may never be broken. East Ridge won the game 38–37, but it took 16 overtime periods for them to do it.

BASKETBALL'S FIRST EARLY BLOOMER

The first player to leave college before graduating and go directly into the pros was Spencer Haywood. Spencer, a 6-foot-9 center/forward, left the University of Detroit as a junior in 1969 and joined the Denver Rockets of the ABA. The NBA, which had a rule that kept teams from signing underclassmen, eventually allowed college players to enter the draft whenever they chose.

Spencer later joined the NBA, first as a member of Seattle SuperSonics. He averaged 30 points per game in the ABA and 19.2 points per game during his NBA career.

KNICKS TRICKS

During the game on November 28, 1969, the New York Knicks' 17–game winning streak looked to be over. The Knicks were trailing the Cincinnati Royals, 105–100, with just 16 seconds left. Then the New Yorkers, known for their team defense, stole the ball from the Royals twice in a row, and scored off both turnovers. The Knicks won the game 106–105 to extend their streak to 18 games, then the longest in NBA history.

WHAT A PISTOL!

The NCAA record for most free throws made in a single game was set in 1969 by Pete Maravich of Louisiana State University. Pete made 30 of 31 shots in a game against Oregon State University.

You've bounded through the story of basketball in the 1960s. Now take a shot at these basketball questions. You can see how well you have scored by checking the answers on page 146.

1 The ABA introduced the three-point shot and the slam-dunk contest to the basketball world. Who won the first slam-dunk contest, in 1976?

2 Oscar Robertson averaged a triple-double per game in his first five NBA seasons. In which triple-double category — scoring, rebounds, or assists — did he lead the NBA six times?

3 Bill Bradley was a college basketball star at Princeton University. He later became a senator from New Jersey. Which former U.S. president played baseball at Yale University?

4 On February 17, 1994, San Antonio Spur center David Robinson became the fourth player to perform a quadruple-double in a game. Where did the player known as "The Admiral" play college basketball?

>> BASKETBALL ROCKS AND ROLLS

1970s

1970 SUPER SHOT

In Game 3 of the 1970 NBA Finals between the Los Angeles Lakers and the New York Knicks, Laker guard Jerry West sank a 65-foot shot as the buzzer sounded to send the game into overtime. New York went on to win the game, and the championship. In today's game, with the three-point field goal, Jerry's shot would have won the game for the Lakers!

NO DOUBT ABOUT IT

Only two players have swept all three MVP Awards — for the All-Star Game, regular season, and NBA Finals — in the same season. Michael Jordan did it during the 1995–96 and 1997–98 seasons. But the first player to pull off that hat trick was Knick center Willis Reed, in 1969–70.

A REAL LONG SHOT

How long was the longest shot ever made? The entire length of the court! It happened in 1970, during an

LEGEND:

KAREEM ABDUL-JABBAR

Kareem Abdul-Jabbar is the NBA's all-time leading scorer, with 38,387 points. He was named MVP six times, more than any other player. He played in more NBA All-Star games (18) during his 20–season career than any other player. But those numbers don't tell the full story about Kareem.

Kareem's parents named him Lew Alcindor, and that's the name by which he first became famous. Lew grew to be 6 feet 4 inches by the time he was 11 years old. He was 6 feet 6 inches when he started high school, at New York City's Power Memorial High. By the time he graduated, he was 7 feet and had grown into a full–size basketball force. He led Power to 71 straight wins.

Lew attended the University of California at Los Angeles. He led UCLA to three national championships and was college Player of the Year three times.

His professional career was just as successful. He earned the NBA's MVP Award in his second season, as he led the Milwaukee Bucks to the NBA title. Lew changed his name to Kareem Abdul-Jabbar in keeping with his Islamic beliefs. But he didn't change his dominating play on the court.

Kareem was traded to the Los Angeles Lakers in 1975. In 1979–80, Magic Johnson joined the Lakers. Together, Kareem and Magic helped Los Angeles win five NBA championships.

These are the numbers that best describe Kareem's career: three high school titles, three college national championships, and six NBA championships.

American Athletics Union (AAU) game at Pacific Lutheran University. A player named Steve Myers threw in a shot while standing out-of-bounds at the opposite end of the court. It was a 92-foot-3-and-a-half-inch shot! (The court was shorter than a regulation-size one, which is 94 feet long.) Since the shot came from out-of-bounds, it shouldn't have counted — but the fans raised such a fuss that officials allowed the basket.

0-FOR-60

In 1971, the Wynot (Nebraska) High School Blue Devils were not a good basketball team. The Blue Devils were in the middle of a 69-game losing streak. Opponents outscored them by an average of 81 points per game during the streak. But on December 10, 1971, the Wynot team was about as bad as a team can be. The team lost a game to Niobrara High School by the embarrassing score of 118–4. Wynot High scored all four of its points from the foul line. The team attempted 60 shots during the game and missed every one!

Field-goal percentage is an important measurement in basketball because it shows how accurate a player is as a shooter. A player's field-goal percentage, or shooting percentage, is the number of shots he makes from the field (every shot except foul shots) compared to the number of shots he takes. In the NBA, any field-goal percentage over .500 is good. A field-goal percentage over .600 is fantastic. The record for a season was set by Wilt Chamberlain, who hit for an amazing .727 in 1972-73.

How do you figure field-goal percentage? It's simple. Divide the number of shots made by the number of shots attempted.

Say a player attempts 17 shots and makes 10 of them. What's his field-goal percentage? Use the formula to the right to help you figure it out. *(Check your answer on page 148.)*

Number of Shots Made
÷
Number of Shots Attempted =
Field-Goal Percentage

After his team's lopsided victory, the Niobrara High coach felt sorry for the losers. "I wanted to run out and shoot a couple of baskets for [Wynot] myself," he said.

1972 FIRST WOMEN'S CHAMPS

The first women's national college championship was won by Immaculata College, a small school outside Philadelphia, Pennsylvania. Immaculata defeated West Chester State (also of Pennsylvania), 52–48, in the first tournament held by the Association for Intercollegiate Athletics for Women (AIAW), in 1972.

Immaculata won the first three AIAW titles. The team was led by three players who went on to be successful women's college coaches: Teresa Shank Grentz, who has coached at Rutgers University, the 1992 U.S. Olympic women's basketball team, and is now at the University of Illinois; Marianne Crawford Stanley, who has coached at five universities and is now an assistant coach with the Washington Mystics of the Women's National Basketball Association (WNBA); and Rene Muth Portland, who coaches Penn State University. In the early 1980s, the NCAA began sponsoring a women's championship tournament, and the AIAW went out of business.

ROUND NUMBER

Elvin Hayes spent 16 seasons in the NBA (1968–84). He played for several different teams. Elvin averaged 21 points per game in 1,303 contests, played in 12 All-Star Games,

and grabbed 16,279 rebounds. But perhaps the most stunning statistic about Elvin is the number of minutes he played in his career — exactly 50,000!

BEST AND WORST

The 1971–72 Los Angeles Lakers, led by Wilt Chamberlain, Jerry West, and Gail Goodrich, had one of the most successful seasons in NBA history. From November 5, 1971 to January 9, 1972, the Lakers won a record 33 games in a row. They finished the regular season with 69 wins, the most ever at the time. (The Chicago Bulls broke the Lakers' record with 72 wins in 1995–96.) The Lakers won 12 of 15 playoff games to win the NBA championship.

One year later, the 1972–73 Philadelphia 76ers produced the *worst* team in league history. After winning only four of their first 51 games, the 76ers fired their coach. But they didn't do much better after that. When the season was over, the Sixers had stumbled to a 9–73 record.

SUPER DAVE

Dave DeBusschere did a little bit of everything in sports. He played major league baseball (he spent two seasons as a pitcher for the Chicago White Sox), and he had played pro basketball with the Detroit Pistons. In 1964, Dave decided to concentrate on basketball full–time. The Pistons made him the team's player–coach. He was just 24 years old and the youngest coach in NBA history.

You are in Munich, West Germany, on September 9, 1972, to watch the U.S. men's basketball team play the Soviet Union team for the Olympic gold medal.

Americans have dominated international basketball up to this point — so you are surprised when, with three seconds left to play, the United States is clinging to a 50–49 lead.

As time runs out, the United States begins to celebrate. But a referee says there is still one second left. Then R. William Jones orders that the clock be reset at three seconds. He is the secretary of the International Amateur Basketball Federation, but he is supposed to be only a spectator, just like you.

The Soviets are given a chance to score with three seconds on the clock. Their shot misses, and the Americans begin hugging again. You start to celebrate, too.

But Mr. Jones interferes again. He says the clock was not reset correctly and the three seconds must be replayed one more time. As you scramble back to your seat, you shake your head in disbelief. You are even more stunned when Soviet player Alexander Belov takes a long pass and scores at the buzzer, giving the Soviet Union a 51–50 victory.

After the game, you find out that the Americans have refused to accept their silver medals. You feel bad about the loss, but you feel even worse for U.S. coach Hank Iba. As he left the court after the game, somebody stole his wallet!

Dave was later traded to the New York Knicks, and helped them win the NBA title in 1970 and 1973. Dave retired and was named commissioner of the ABA in 1976. Dave went on to serve as the Knicks' general manager, a position he held when the team drafted Patrick Ewing in 1985.

AN ALMOST PERFECT DAY

Bill Walton had perhaps the best big-game performance in college basketball history. On March 26, 1973, Bill's UCLA team faced Memphis State University in the championship game of the NCAA tournament. Bill led the Bruins to an 87–66 victory — and their seventh straight NCAA title — by scoring more than half of his team's points! He poured in 44 points, including an amazing 21 field goals in 22 attempts.

Bill's great day was no fluke. The 6-foot-11 center was a three-time college Player of the Year from 1972 to 1974. He was the NBA's MVP in 1978, when he played with the Portland Trail Blazers.

LEGEND:

PETE MARAVICH

Pete Maravich first picked up a basketball at the age of seven and hardly ever put it down after that. He went on to become the highest scoring college player ever. His nickname was "Pistol Pete" because he could really shoot. Pete scored more points in his three varsity seasons at Louisiana State University (3,667) than any other player has scored in four seasons of college basketball.

Pete led the nation in scoring in each of those three seasons. In fact, his points per game averages of 44.5 (1969–70), 44.2 (1968–69), and 43.8 (1967–68) are the top three marks in NCAA Division I history.

But Pete could do more than shoot. He was an exciting passer and dribbler, and a great showman. He made no-look passes and dribbled through and around defenders to get open for shots.

"If I have a choice whether to do the show or throw the straight pass and we're going to get the basket either way, I'm going to do the show," Pete once explained. His trademark was a pair of floppy socks that he wore in every game.

After college, Pete joined the NBA. He averaged 24.2 points per game for 10 seasons. He led the league in scoring once and made the All-Star team four times.

Pete retired in 1980, but he never lost his love for basketball. He died of a heart attack in 1988 at the age of 40, while playing a pickup game in a church gym.

Bill also did well in the sixth game of the 1977 NBA Finals. He had 20 points, 23 rebounds, seven assists, and eight blocked shots against the Philadelphia 76ers. The Trail Blazers won the game — and their first NBA title.

THE STREAK IS SHOT DOWN

The UCLA Bruins had won a record 88 straight games when the team traveled to South Bend, Indiana, to face the University of Notre Dame. It was January 19, 1974. The year before, UCLA had crushed Notre Dame, 114–56. The Fighting Irish wanted nothing more than to stop the Bruins' streak.

It didn't look promising for the Fighting Irish, as UCLA led, 70–59, late in the game. Then an amazing thing happened. Notre Dame scored the last 12 points of the game, including a last-second jump shot by Dwight Clay that gave the Irish a 71–70 lead. Notre Dame won, and the Bruins' great run was over.

THE BLAZE

When women's college basketball began to take off in the 1970s, one of the first great stars was Carol Blazejowski of Montclair State College in New Jersey. "The Blaze," as she was called, set women's basketball on fire. In her three seasons on the Montclair varsity, Carol averaged 31.7 points per game.

THE WIZ

John Wooden is the only person ever elected to the Basketball Hall of Fame as a player and as a coach. In 1961, he was voted in as a player. He had been a three-time all-America at Purdue University in the 1930s. In 1932, he was the college Player of the Year.

As coach of the UCLA men's basketball team, John was called the "Wizard of Westwood." (Westwood is the suburb of Los Angeles in which UCLA is located.) His teams won 10 NCAA championships from 1964 through 1975, and had four seasons with a perfect record of 30–0. The 10 titles are twice as many as any other coach in history.

FAST BREAK

Only one person in NBA history has ever led the league in both scoring and assists in the same season. Playing for the Kansas City-Omaha Kings, Nate "Tiny" Archibald averaged 34 points and 11.4 assists per game in 1972-73. That meant Nate had a hand in about 56 of his team's points every night! By the way, the 6-foot-1 Nate became the shortest scoring champion (at the time) in league history.

Coach Wooden was elected to the Hall of Fame again in 1972, this time as the most successful coach in college basketball history. After the 1975 championship, he stepped down from coaching while he was still on top.

1976 DUNK FUNK

In 1976, a player for Mississippi State University named Wiley Peck dunked the basketball so hard that the ball hit him in the face coming through the net and knocked him out. He was unconscious for two minutes.

THE LONGEST CHAMPIONSHIP GAME

The Boston Celtics and the Phoenix Suns played the longest game in NBA Finals history in 1976. The game started on June 4 and ended on June 5. It lasted four hours and 20 seconds. The Celtics won, 128–126, in the third overtime, after midnight.

GOLDEN OPPORTUNITIES

The first Olympic gold medal in women's basketball was won by the Soviet Union in 1976. The United States won the silver medal. The U.S. women's basketball team won its first gold medal in basketball in 1984.

On May 8, 1970, the Los Angeles Lakers and the New York Knicks met in Game 7 of the NBA Finals at Madison Square Garden in New York City. The teams had split the first six games of the series.

Knick captain Willis Reed injured his leg in Game 5 and wasn't able to play in Game 6. It was doubtful that Willis, the team captain, would play in the final game. But, at the start of the game, he hobbled onto the court with his leg bandaged. He was going to play. The New York fans went wild, especially when Willis scored the first two field goals of the game.

The Knick center provided the inspiration, and guard Walt Frazier supplied everything else, with 36 points and 19 assists. Fueled by one of the most dramatic moments in league history, the Knicks won the championship with a 113–99 victory.

WHAT'S IN A NAME?

During the 1976–77 season, the Detroit Pistons were rich with players named Eric Money and Cornelius Cash. The Seattle SuperSonics had colorful teammates named Michael Green, Leonard Gray, and Fred Brown.

1978 SCORING WAR

As the 1977–78 season wound down, two players — Denver's David Thompson and San Antonio's George Gervin — were battling it out for the NBA scoring title. George was averaging 26.78 points per game going into the final afternoon of the season. David's average was 26.57 points per game.

In his final game of the season, David scored an astonishing 73 points. That raised his scoring average to 27.15. George needed to score 58 points in his final game that night to regain the lead. Too much pressure? Not for the player known as the "Iceman." George went out and scored 63 points. He captured the first of his four NBA scoring titles with an average of 27.21 points per game.

NUMBERS GAME

Rick Barry had always worn number 24 as a pro. But when Rick joined the Houston Rockets in 1978, Moses Malone was already wearing 24. So Rick and the Rockets came up with a solution. He wore number 2 during home games and number 4 on the road.

TRADING PLACES

On November 8, 1978, the Philadelphia 76ers apparently defeated the New Jersey Nets, 137–133. But the Nets protested the game because of an official's call. The last part of the game was replayed more than four months later. When the game resumed, two 76er players and one Net player were on opposite sides. They had been traded for each other. No matter. The Sixers won again, 123–117.

1979 NOT READY FOR PRIME TIME

Dick Vitale is best known today as a college basketball commentator on television. But in 1978–79, he coached the NBA's Detroit Pistons. (He also coached on the college level, at the University of Detroit.) Dick's Pistons didn't win their first game until the sixth contest of the season. But Dick wasn't around to enjoy his first NBA victory. He had been ejected from the game.

The Pistons finished 30–52 that season. Dick was fired 12 games into the following season.

DR. DUNKENSTEIN

Darryl Dawkins, the 6–foot–10, 260–pound center for the Philadelphia 76ers, New Jersey Nets, and Detroit Pistons, had a nickname for himself: Chocolate Thunder. He was also known as "Dr. Dunkenstein."

Darryl was famous for shattering backboards with his thunderous dunks. He liked to name his dunks, too. He called them names such as "Earthquaker Shaker," "Turbo Delight," "In–Your–Face Disgrace," and "Spine–Chiller Supreme."

In 1979, Darryl shattered two backboards within 22 days. One time, he broke the glass while dunking over Bill Robinzine of the Kansas City Kings with his

The greatest college basketball team of all time was Coach John Wooden's UCLA Bruins from 1964 to 1975.

UCLA seemed to own the NCAA tournament, winning an incredible 10 national titles in 12 seasons, including seven in a row!

The Bruins started their championship streak with the 1964-65 season, when they went 30–0 and won the national title. The following year, they repeated as champions.

After one off-season, UCLA came back strong. Led by 7-foot-2 center Lew Alcindor (Kareem Abdul-Jabbar), the Bruins won three straight national championships.

UCLA won two more titles, in 1970 and 1971, and then another dominant center arrived on campus — Bill Walton. Over three seasons with Bill, UCLA won 88 games in a row! That included national titles in 1972 and 1973. Two years later, UCLA won its 10th and last title under Coach Wooden.

"Chocolate–Thunder Flyin', Robinzine–Cryin', Teeth–
Shakin', Glass–Breakin', Rump–Roastin', Sun–Toastin',
Wham, Bam, Glass–Breaker–I–Am Jam."

LAND OF THE FREE . . . THROW

The longest free–throw shooting streak in actual games,
rather than shooting exhibitions, doesn't belong to a pro,
or even to a college player. That record is owned by Daryl
Moreau of de LaSalle High, in New Orleans, Louisiana.
Over two seasons, Daryl made 126 free throws in a row.

THE CBA IS BORN

In 1978–79, a minor pro league called the Eastern
Basketball Association changed its name to the Continental
Basketball Association (CBA). In 1980, the CBA signed an
agreement with the NBA to be its official minor league
and help develop players for the NBA. That means
players who might have a future in the NBA can spend
a season or two in the CBA improving their skills.

Many successful NBA players got their starts in the
CBA. John Starks, Anthony Mason, and more than 500
other players have gone from the CBA to the NBA.

LAND OF THE THREE

The first season of the three–point field goal in the
NBA was 1979–80. The league first set the distance for the
extra–credit field goal at 23 feet nine inches. At the start

of the 1994–95 season, the NBA reduced the three–point distance to 22 feet. Then, before the 1997–98 season, it was moved back to 23 feet nine inches again. (The three–point distance in college basketball is 19 feet nine inches. In international competition, such as the Olympic Games, the three–point line is 20 feet six inches from the basket.)

BIRD MEETS MAGIC

On March 26, 1979, two of the greatest players in basketball history met on the basketball court for the first time. It was the start of a rivalry between Magic Johnson and Larry Bird that would last until they retired from the pros in the early 1990s.

Both were great college players. Magic attended college at Michigan State University, and Larry went to Indiana State University. Both stars led their teams to the 1979 NCAA Final Four and then to the championship game.

The whole country seemed to be watching as the nation's top two players battled it out. The game was seen on

LEGEND:

ANN MEYERS

Ann Meyers achieved a lot of "firsts" in her basketball career. After competing in volleyball, softball, tennis, track and field, field hockey, and badminton in high school, she became the first woman to receive a full athletic scholarship from the University of California at Los Angeles.

At UCLA, Ann became the first four-time All-America in women's basketball history. She averaged 17.4 points and 8.4 rebounds per game. In 1978, her senior year, she led UCLA to the national championship and was college Player of the Year. (Ann's brother David starred on the 1975 UCLA national champion men's team, and on the NBA's Milwaukee Bucks.) Ann held 12 school records at UCLA.

In 1976, Ann competed on the first U.S. Olympic Women's Basketball Team, earning a silver medal. In 1979, she became the first woman to sign a free-agent contract with an NBA team (the Indiana Pacers). She played for the New Jersey Gems in the Women's Professional Basketball League and was named its first MVP.

After Ann's athletic career ended, she became a sports broadcaster. In 1986, she married Baseball Hall of Famer Don Drysdale. A former pitcher, Don was also working as a sports broadcaster.

In 1993, Ann was elected to the Basketball Hall of Fame. That gave her another first. She and Don were the first married couple to both be members of sports halls of fame.

television by more people than any other game in college basketball history. Michigan State won, 75–64. And Magic outscored Larry, 24–19.

Magic and Larry met on the court many times after that game. The following season, Magic joined the Los Angeles Lakers and Larry went to work for the Boston Celtics. During their pro careers, they met in the NBA Finals three times. Magic and the Lakers won twice. In 1992, they finally got to play together as teammates, on the U.S. Olympic Dream Team.

OVERTIME

By now you probably know a little bit about basketball in the 1970s. But what do you know about basketball today? Answer these questions. Then check your score on page 147.

UCLA won seven straight NCAA championships from 1967 to 1973. What school was the next team to win back-to-back titles? *(Hint: The next team won in 1991 and 1992.)*

Kareem Abdul-Jabbar is 7 feet 2 inches tall. How many inches is that?

Pistol Pete Maravich was the "big man" at Louisiana State University in the late 1960s. What current NBA big man starred at LSU in the early 1990s?

At 6 feet 1 inch, Nate Archibald became the shortest scoring champion in NBA history. What 6-foot guard led the NBA in scoring, playing for the Philadelphia 76ers, in 2000-01?

>> MAGIC TIME

1980s

1980 POINT CENTER

The NBA has some decent-sized point guards today. Jason Kidd is 6 feet 4 inches. Steve Nash is 6 feet 3 inches. Andre Miller is 6 feet 2 inches. But Magic Johnson — at 6 feet 9 inches — was the league's first big point guard. A few years before he joined the NBA, a player his size would have been playing center.

On May 16, 1980, Magic was asked to do just that. His team, the Los Angeles Lakers, was playing the Philadelphia 76ers in the NBA Finals. The Lakers led, three games to two. But Laker center Kareem Abdul-Jabbar was injured and had to sit out Game 6.

Magic, a rookie point guard, moved over to play center. He scored 42 points, grabbed 15 rebounds, and dished out seven assists. The Lakers won the game, 123–107, and the NBA title.

FRESH FACE

In the championship game of the 1982 NCAA tournament, the North Carolina Tar Heels played the Georgetown Hoyas at the New Orleans Superdome. The teams faced off in front of 66,612 people.

North Carolina got off to an 8–0 lead — without the ball going through the basket even once! Georgetown center Patrick Ewing swatted away four straight Tar Heel shots. But he was called for goaltending each time, so North Carolina got the points.

Still, the Hoyas were ahead, 32–31 at halftime. The two teams then traded the lead for the rest of the game — until the last 18 seconds. That's when a freshman guard for North Carolina hit a 16–foot jump shot to give his team the national title. The guard's name? Michael Jordan.

ONE THAT GOT AWAY

Michael Jordan turned pro in 1984. Believe it or not, he was not the first college player drafted in that year's NBA draft. He wasn't even the second. The Houston Rockets had the first pick. They took 7–foot center Hakeem Olajuwon of the University of Houston. The Portland Trail Blazers drafted 7–foot center Sam Bowie of the University of Kentucky. The Chicago Bulls, who had a 27–55 record in 1983–84, drafted Michael with the third pick of the draft.

LEGEND:

JULIUS ERVING

Even Michael Jordan had an idol when he was a kid. He was Julius Erving, known to the basketball world as "Doctor J." No one is sure who gave Julius the nickname — he probably got it on a playground in Roosevelt, New York, where he grew up — but it fit him perfectly.

Julius was a 6–foot–7 forward with huge hands. He soared through the air like no player had done before him, making spectacular dunks, passes, and rebounds. And he did it all with grace and dignity. Julius didn't do anything to show off, only to help his team win the game.

After spending two years at the University of Massachusetts, Julius began his pro career with the Virginia Squires of the American Basketball Association in 1971. He led the league in scoring three times and was named the league MVP three seasons in a row. As a member of the New York Nets, Julius helped lift his team to two championships.

After the ABA and NBA merged in 1976, Julius was traded to the Philadelphia 76ers. He spent 11 seasons with the Sixers, averaging more than 20 points per game and appearing in 11 All–Star Games. In 1981, he was the league's Most Valuable Player. In 1983, he and super center Moses Malone led the 76ers to the NBA title.

FEMALE FIRSTS

Who was the first woman to dunk in a college game? It was 6–foot–7 center Georgeann Wells of the University of Charleston (West Virginia). She did it in 1984. Lynette Woodard, who was an All–America at Kansas University, became the first woman to play for the Harlem Globetrotters, in 1985.

1985 THE BIG UPSET

The final game of the 1985 NCAA tournament seemed like a mismatch. Georgetown University, led by Patrick Ewing, was playing Villanova University. Georgetown was the defending national champion and had a 35–2 record going into the game. Villanova was 25–10.

Before the game, Villanova coach Rollie Massimino said, "To win it, we've really got to play a perfect game." The Villanova Wildcats weren't perfect, but they were close enough. They hit nearly 80 percent of their shots and squeaked out a 66–64 victory. Villanova became the third team ever to win the national title after having as many as 10 losses.

Several years later, Coach Massimino said that he had a videotape of the game, but rarely watched it. Why?

"Because I still think we're going to lose," he said.

INDOOR RAIN

Would you believe that an NBA game could be rained out? That's what happened in Seattle, Washington, on January 5, 1986. The SuperSonics were playing the Phoenix Suns. Holes in the roof of the arena left puddles on the floor! The game was postponed in the middle of the second period. It was continued the next day. This time the sun beat the rain, and the Sonics beat the Suns.

The San Antonio Spurs' 1994–95 season got off to a soggy beginning. The season opener against the Golden State Warriors started with a real bang: an indoor fireworks display. Then, all of a sudden, *splash!*

FAST BREAK

In a span of four seasons, between 1976 and 1980, Magic Johnson was named the Most Valuable Player of his state high school championship, the NCAA Tournament, and the NBA championship series.

Rebounding average measures the number of rebounds a player grabs in a typical game. In the NBA today, an average of more than 10 rebounds per game is considered very good.

A player's rebounding average is equal to the number of rebounds he has grabbed, divided by the total number of games he has played. For example, if a player grabs 39 rebounds in three games, his rebound average is 39 divided by three, or 13 rebounds per game.

Say a player plays in six games, and his rebound totals are 10, 12, 8, 6, 12, and 11. What is his rebounding average? Use the formula to help figure it out. *(Check your answer on page 148.)*

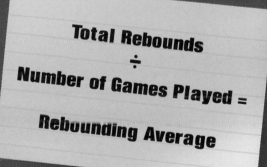

Total Rebounds
÷
Number of Games Played =
Rebounding Average

The fireworks had triggered the sprinkler system in the Alamodome. Fifty minutes and nearly 150,000 gallons of water later, the game got under way.

A GULP OF AIR

Michael Jordan missed all but 18 games during the 1985–86 NBA season with a broken foot, but he was back in shape for the playoffs. Boy, was he ever! Against the Boston Celtics on April 20, 1986, Michael broke a 34-year-old playoff record by pouring in 63 points. Elgin Baylor had set the previous record of 61 points in 1962 — also against the Celtics.

LEAPING LIEBERMAN

Nancy Lieberman was a 5-foot-10 guard who led Old Dominion University to national championships in 1979 and 1980. After both seasons, she was named college Player of the Year.

In 1976, Nancy was the youngest member of the first U.S. Olympic Women's Basketball Team. She was 16 years old. After college, she played one season in the pro Women's Basketball League.

LEGEND:

LARRY BIRD

Larry Bird wasn't exceptionally big or fast or even a great jumper. But he made himself into one of the greatest forwards in basketball history.

Larry grew up in the small town of French Lick, Indiana. His family was poor, but he was rich in basketball talent. Larry grew to 6 feet 9 inches. He became a great shooter, rebounder, and passer, as well as a dedicated team player.

In college, Larry averaged 30.1 points per game. During the 1978–79 season, he led little Indiana State University to the Number 1 ranking in the country and to the championship game of the NCAA tournament. Larry's team lost the title game to Magic Johnson's Michigan State team.

Larry joined the NBA's Boston Celtics in 1979. The team had been losing and Larry immediately helped them become winners. He was named the NBA Rookie of the Year. In his second season, Larry led the Celtics to the NBA championship. It was the first of three championships they won in his first seven seasons in the pros. He averaged 24 points, 10 rebounds, and six assists per game in his 13–season career, earning three straight MVP Awards from 1984 to 1986.

Back trouble forced Larry to retire early from the NBA, but not before he had accomplished one last thing on the court. In 1992, Larry co–captained the Dream Team to a gold medal at the Summer Olympics. It was the perfect way for a true winner to end his career.

LAKERS VS. CELTICS

The Boston Celtics have won 16 NBA titles, while the Lakers (in Minneapolis and Los Angeles) have won 13. No other team has won so many titles. Such great performances fueled a great rivalry between the teams.

Over the years, the Celtics and the Lakers have featured some of the most talented players ever. Boston has had Bob Cousy, Bill Russell, John Havlicek, Larry Bird, and Kevin McHale. The Lakers have boasted George Mikan, Elgin Baylor, Jerry West, Wilt Chamberlain, Kareem Abdul-Jabbar, Magic Johnson, and James Worthy. Thanks to these great players, the teams have faced each other in the NBA Finals 10 times.

The first time the two teams met for the league championship was in 1959. The Celtics swept the Lakers four games to zero. In the 1960s, the two teams squared off for the league title six times in eight years (in 1962, 1963, 1965, 1966, 1968, and 1969) — and the Celtics won every time.

The Lakers and Celtics didn't meet again in the Finals until 1984. Larry Bird's Celtics slipped past Magic Johnson's Lakers, four games to three.

The next season, Magic and the Lakers returned the favor, winning the 1985 championship. In 1987, Larry and Magic led their teams to the Finals for the third time. The Lakers were victorious, four games to two, but the fans were the real winners.

In 1986, Nancy played in a game between the Springfield Fame and the Staten Island Stallions of the United States Basketball League. She played only three minutes, but made history: She was the first woman to compete in a men's pro game.

1987 SMART SHOT

In the championship game of the 1987 NCAA tournament, Syracuse University led Indiana University, 73–72, late in the game. With time running out, Indiana's Keith Smart connected on a 16-foot jump shot from the left baseline to give his team a 74–73 victory. It was Indiana's fourth national championship, and the Hoosiers' third NCAA title in 12 seasons under legendary coach Bob Knight.

FAST BREAK

Bob Lanier, a 6-foot-11 Hall of Famer, spent 14 seasons in the NBA with the Detroit Pistons and Milwaukee Bucks. His career scoring average was an impressive 20.1 points per game, but it didn't match his shoe size. Bob's feet were size 22. (Shaquille O'Neal also wears a size 22.)

HERE COMES JORDAN

How dominant was Michael Jordan during the 1987–88 season? He won the NBA scoring title, averaging 37.1 points per game, and was given the Most Valuable Player Award. But Michael did not stop there. He also led the league in steals, averaging 3.16 per game and was named Defensive Player of the Year.

To top it off, Michael was the All–Star Game MVP. In front of his home crowd in Chicago, he scored 40 points and led the East All–Stars to victory. Michael also won the Slam Dunk Championship for the second year in a row.

GOOD MOURNING!

In 1988, Alonzo Mourning, then a high school senior in Chesapeake, Virginia, blocked 29 shots in one game. Alonzo's amazing effort came during an Amateur Athletics Union tournament. Alonzo led the nation in blocks the following year as a college freshman at Georgetown University.

LEGEND:

MAGIC JOHNSON

Earvin "Magic" Johnson seemed to have a lot of fun playing basketball — and winning.

Earvin grew up in East Lansing, Michigan, as one of 10 children. He learned to dribble and pass as a way to get chosen in playground basketball games. An announcer at one of his high school games nicknamed him "Magic" because of the magical things Earvin could do on the court.

By the time he entered college, Magic was 6 feet 9 inches and the tallest point guard anyone had ever seen. Nobody could believe that a person that tall could handle the ball that well. Magic led the NBA in assists four times. His 10,141 career assists rank second in league history.

Magic could also score and rebound. The triple–double statistic (when a player reaches double figures in three statistical categories in one game) was created partly because of him.

Magic teamed with Kareem Abdul–Jabbar to lead the Lakers to five NBA titles. Magic was named league MVP three times. He retired from the NBA in 1991 after he discovered that he had HIV, the virus that causes AIDS. His announcement saddened his many fans all over the world.

Magic returned to basketball as co–captain of the U.S. Dream Team at the 1992 Summer Olympics. He also played 32 games for the Lakers at the end of the 1995–96 NBA regular season.

FLIP SIDE

John Stockton of the Utah Jazz recorded 24 assists in a playoff game against the Los Angeles Lakers on May 17, 1988. In doing so, John tied a playoff record. The record had been set by the man who was guarding John that day — Magic Johnson.

KID NAMES THAT STUCK

Anthony "Spud" Webb was only 5 feet 7 inches. But his nickname has nothing to do with his size, or with potatoes. When Spud was a baby, his brothers and sisters decided that his head looked like *Sputnik*. That was the name of a spacecraft launched by the Soviet Union a few years earlier. But some of the Webb kids could not pronounce *Sputnik*. Instead, it came out "Spud." Anthony's size didn't hold him back from achieving big things: In 1986, he won the NBA Slam Dunk contest.

Dennis "Worm" Rodman's nickname had nothing to do with the way he snaked under the basket for rebounds. His nickname also came from his childhood. Dennis's friends called him "Worm" because of the way he wriggled when he played pinball! Dennis was one of the toughest defenders and rebounders in the NBA in the 1980s and 1990s.

PERFECT COACH

Two days before the 1989 NCAA men's tournament, assistant coach Steve Fisher took over as head coach of the University of Michigan. Coach Fisher had never been head coach of a college team. It did not matter. Michigan won the NCAA championship.

Coach Fisher had captured the national title without losing a game.

ONE-WOMAN SHOW

On February 16, 1989, Dawn Moss became the only person in basketball history to outscore her own team. How? The 5-foot-7 senior from Steward School, in Virginia, scored all of her own team's points. She also accidentally scored a basket for her opponent! Steward beat Tappahannock St. Margaret's in overtime, 47–45. Dawn scored 49 points.

OVERTIME

It's time to test your basketball smarts once again. Check your score on page 147.

Magic Johnson broke Oscar Robertson's career record for most assists in NBA history. Who broke Magic's record in February 1995 by dishing out his 9,922nd career assist?

Manute Bol, the first 7-foot-7 player in NBA history, is from Africa. Another center from Africa won the NBA's Most Valuable Player Award in 1994. Name that player.

Georgetown University, the NBA's Wizards, and the United States Senate all call the same city home. Can you name the city?

Michigan won the 1989 NCAA championship with an overtime victory over Seton Hall. The next NCAA championship overtime game was played in 1997. The University of Kentucky Wildcats lost to another school whose nickname is the Wildcats. What team beat Kentucky in the 1997 NCAA championship game?

>> BASKETBALL TODAY

1990s and 2000s

1990 HOOPS 101

Lisa Leslie, a 6-foot-5 senior player at Morningside High School, in Inglewood, California, scored 101 points in the first half of a 1990 game against South Torrance High School. But Lisa didn't get a chance to break the modern single-game high school record of 105 points.

The record had been set in 1982, by Cheryl Miller of Riverside Poly High School, in California.

Several South Torrance players had been injured and others had been called for many fouls in the first half. They would have had to play the second half with just four players. So Lisa's team decided not to finish the game, leaving Lisa with a very unusual record.

SIXTH MAN

You never know who you'll run into on the basketball court. In a 1991 game between the Denver Nuggets and the Milwaukee Bucks, Denver guard Michael Adams was

dribbling downcourt when he ran into a man who was *not* one of the players. He was one of the Bucks, though.

The obstacle on the court was Bucks then-head coach, Del Harris. He had walked onto the court to argue a referee's call. Coach Harris was ejected from the game and slapped with a $1,000 fine.

WHAT A FINISH!

Grant Hill and Christian Laettner were teammates on the Detroit Pistons in 1999. As teammates at Duke University, they created one of the most exciting finishes in college hoops history.

Duke was facing the University of Kentucky on March 28, 1992, in the East Regional finals of the NCAA tournament. The winner would go to the Final Four. The lead went back and forth until Kentucky led 103–102, with just 2.1 seconds remaining. Duke had enough time for a last-ditch attempt.

Grant stood out-of-bounds under Kentucky's basket and threw the ball as hard as he could toward the other basket. It flew 75 feet, straight into Christian's hands. Christian dribbled left, spun, and sank the game-winning shot as the buzzer sounded. Duke went on to win the national championship, its second in a row.

DREAM TEAMS

The United States Olympic Basketball Team used to be made up mostly of college players. But in 1992, professionals were allowed to compete at the Summer Olympics for the first time. The 12 players representing the United States. At those Games were Larry Bird, Magic Johnson, David Robinson, Michael Jordan, Patrick Ewing, Charles Barkley, Clyde Drexler, Karl Malone, John Stockton, Chris Mullin, Scottie Pippen, and Christian Laettner. The United States easily won the gold medal. No wonder they were called the Dream Team.

Two years later, another team of NBA stars was put together to compete in the 1994 World Championships of Basketball. This team also won the gold. Dream Team II, as the squad was called, included Shaquille O'Neal, Reggie Miller, and other NBA stars. Dream Team III won a gold medal at the 1996 Summer Olympics in Atlanta, Georgia. Grant Hill, Karl Malone and Scottie Pippen were among the players on that team.

FAST BREAK

Michael Jordan was still true to his school, the University of North Carolina, even while he was playing for the Chicago Bulls. When he dressed for games, Michael put on blue Carolina shorts under his Chicago uniform.

By the way, Michael got his habit of sticking out his tongue while playing from his dad, who used to do the same thing while he was working in the family's yard.

LEGEND:

MICHAEL JORDAN

When people say Michael Jordan is the best to ever play the game of basketball, it's hard to argue with them.

Michael attended the University of North Carolina, where he became famous as a freshman by hitting the 16-foot jump shot that gave the Tar Heels the 1982 national championship. He was named college Player of the Year in his sophomore and junior seasons at North Carolina, then joined the Chicago Bulls in 1984. He promptly became the NBA Rookie of the Year. After that, Michael only got better.

Michael has led the NBA in scoring 10 times. He has averaged a record 31.5 points per game in his career. He also holds playoff records of 33.4 points per game for his career and 63 points in a single game. Michael led the Bulls to three straight NBA championships, from 1991–93, before retiring to pursue a baseball career.

When baseball didn't work out, Michael returned to the NBA at the end of the 1994–95 season. He led the Bulls to three more NBA championships, from 1996 to 1998. He came back from his second retirement in 2001–02, to play for the Washington Wizards.

Michael earned league MVP honors in 1988, 1991, 1992, 1996, and 1998. He was MVP of the NBA Finals all six times the Bulls won the championship. He also earned Olympic gold medals in 1984 and 1992. Not bad for a player who once was cut from his high school team.

Dream Team IV kept the United States on a winning streak by taking the gold medal at the 2000 Summer Olympics in Sydney, Australia. Vince Carter, Kevin Garnett, and Alonzo Mourning were some of the players on the U.S. squad. It was the twelfth gold medal in 14 Olympic basketball competitions for the United States.

1993 FATHER KNOWS BEST

When Hofstra University played Cornell University on January 12, 1993, a father and son roamed each sideline. Hofstra was coached by Butch van Breda Kolff, while Cornell was coached by Butch's son, Jan. The van Breda Kolffs were the third father–son combination to face off in an NCAA Division I game.

Ray Meyer, of DePaul University, and his son Tom, of the University of Illinois–Chicago, coached against each other in 1981. Before that, Ed Diddle, of Western Kentucky, and Ed Junior, of Middle Tennessee State, faced each other 12 times between 1957 and 1962. By the way, the father has won 12 of 14 father–son games.

Steals average measures how many steals a player gets in a typical game. In the NBA, an average greater than two is outstanding. The single-season record in the NBA is held by Alvin Robertson. He averaged 3.67 steals per game for the San Antonio Spurs during the 1985-86 season.

To figure steals average, divide the total number of steals a player has recorded by the number of games he has played in. For example, if a player has 15 steals in 12 games, his steals average is 15 (number of steals) divided by 12 (number of games), or 1.25 steals per game.

If a player competes in four games, and his steals totals are 3, 4, 1, and 1, what is his steals average? You can use this formula to figure it out. *(Check your answer on page 148.)*

Number of Steals

÷

Number of Games Played =

Steals Average

LOST IN TIME

Chris Webber had been the best player on the court for the University of Michigan Wolverines as they battled North Carolina in the championship game of the 1993 NCAA tournament. He would finish with 23 points and 11 rebounds. With 46 seconds remaining, Michigan called for a timeout. The Wolverines trailed, 72–69, and the team's coaches reminded everyone that they had no more timeouts left.

Chris scored the next basket, and Michigan trailed by one point. North Carolina then made one free throw and missed the second. The Wolverines trailed by two points, with 20 seconds left. Chris rebounded the missed foul shot and started up the court. Suddenly, right in front of the Michigan bench, he put his hands together to call a timeout.

The North Carolina bench jumped up. Chris had forgotten that Michigan didn't have any timeouts left. It's a violation to call a timeout when you don't have any. North Carolina was allowed to shoot two technical foul shots. The Tar Heels sank both of them. Carolina later made two more free throws and won the national title, 77–71.

THREE-PEAT!

The Chicago Bulls won the NBA title in 1991, 1992, and 1993, becoming the first team to win three straight since the Boston Celtics of the 1960s. The Bulls defeated the Los Angeles Lakers for the 1991 NBA championship.

They went on to win two more crowns, beating the Portland Trail Blazers in 1992 and the Phoenix Suns in 1993.

Sportswriters sometimes jokingly referred to the Chicago Bulls as "Michael and the Jordanaires." Why? Because during most of those years, the team was led by three players: Michael; power forward Horace Grant, a player known for his defense and rebounding; and small forward Scottie Pippen, an all-around threat who was named to the 1992 Dream Team.

Of course, the most important Bull was Michael. Since the NBA Finals MVP Award was first given out in 1969, no player had ever won it two years in a row — until Michael won it three straight times.

GAME NAME

In 1993, there were 13 players in the NBA with the last name of Williams — and none of them were related! They were Brian Williams, Buck Williams, Corey Williams, Herb Williams, Jayson Williams, John "Hot Rod" Williams, John "Hot Plate" Williams, Kenny Williams, Lorenzo Williams, Michael Williams, Reggie Williams, Scott Williams, and Walt Williams.

"I wouldn't want my last name to be anything else," Kenny said. "Except maybe *Jordan*."

MICHAEL SAYS GOOD-BYE

October 6, 1993, was a sad day for basketball fans around the world. That was the day Michael Jordan announced his retirement. He said there was nothing left for him to prove, and he was retiring from basketball the way he had always wanted to: on top.

Michael didn't stay away from competitive sports for long. Four months after his retirement from hoops, he took batting practice with the Chicago White Sox. Michael had always dreamed of playing professional baseball. But he had not played organized ball since 1981, when he was a senior in high school.

In February 1994, Michael reported to the Chicago White Sox spring-training camp, in Sarasota, Florida. His baseball skills needed plenty of work. The White Sox sent him to the Birmingham Barons, their Class AA minor league team, in Alabama. He started in rightfield and batted .202, with three homers, 51 RBIs, and 30 stolen bases.

FAST BREAK

Center Shaquille O'Neal is famous for scoring, rebounding, blocking shots, and battering backboards. In a February 1993 game against the Phoenix Suns, Shaq dunked so hard that the basket support collapsed. Just two months later, in a game against the New Jersey Nets, another powerful Shaq dunk brought the hoop and the 24-second clock crashing down on top of him!

LEGEND:

CHARLES BARKLEY

Charles Barkley is one of the most outrageous and outspoken players in NBA history. ("I am not a role model," he once said.) But he's also one of the most outstanding.

Charles was only 6 feet 4 inches tall, but he was a great rebounder and inside scorer. In his first 14 seasons as a pro, Charles averaged 22.5 points, 11.7 rebounds, and 3.9 assists per game.

Charles started playing basketball when he was nine, in his hometown of Leeds, Alabama. He didn't make his high school varsity team until his junior year. He worked hard and earned a scholarship to play basketball at Auburn University, in Alabama. He was chosen the Southeastern Conference Player of the Year after his junior year and later was named the SEC Player of the Decade for the 1980s.

Charles joined the NBA in 1984, and spent his first eight seasons in Philadelphia, where he led the 76ers to the playoffs six times. He was traded to the Phoenix Suns in 1992, and led the Suns to the NBA Finals in his first season with the team. He scored 56 points in one playoff game, the third–highest mark in NBA playoff history. Charles also won the league's Most Valuable Player Award, after averaging 25.6 points and 12.2 rebounds per game during the season.

Charles played four seasons with the Suns before being traded to the Houston Rockets. He helped lead the Rockets to the 1997 Western Conference Finals but once again fell short of his ultimate goal: an NBA title.

On March 10, 1995, Michael retired from minor league baseball. Less than two weeks later, he made millions of basketball fans happy with two little words: "I'm back."

1996 THE NBA TURNS 50

The NBA celebrated its 50th season in 1996–97. On October 29, 1996, it announced the 50 Greatest Players in NBA History, as selected by a panel of sportswriters, former players, coaches, and team executives.

The 50th Anniversary All-Time Team included NBA legends such as Michael Jordan, Kareem Abdul-Jabbar, Magic Johnson, Larry Bird, Julius "Dr. J" Erving, Wilt Chamberlain, Jerry West, Oscar Robertson, Bill Walton, and Pete Maravich. It also included eight players who were still active when the 1999 season began: Shaquille O'Neal, Charles Barkley, Scottie Pippen, John Stockton, Patrick Ewing, Hakeem Olajuwon, David Robinson, and Karl Malone.

The 50 players have a combined total of 112 NBA championships, 51 MVP awards, 17 Rookie-of-the-Year awards, and 38 scoring titles. The greats also combined for more than 450 All–Star Game selections, nearly one million points scored, and more than 400,000 rebounds.

WHAT A PAIR!

Karl Malone and John Stockton of the Utah Jazz form one of the best one–two punches in NBA history. The two All–Stars have been teammates since the 1985–86 season and have helped each other into the record books.

Karl is known to NBA fans as The Mailman because he "always delivers" with his play. Karl is the only NBA player to score at least 2,000 points in a season in 11 straight seasons.

On February 1, 1995, John made a special delivery of his own. He flipped a pass to Karl for an easy basket. With that pass, John broke the NBA record for most assists. It was his 9,922nd.

Karl and John were named co–MVPs of the 1993 NBA All–Star Game, which was played in their home arena in Salt Lake City, Utah. In 1996, they were named to the NBA's 50th Anniversary All–Time Team. Together.

THREE-PEAT REPEAT!

Michael Jordan came out of retirement from basketball late in the 1994–95 season. But the Bulls lost to Shaquille O'Neal and the Orlando Magic in the best–of–seven

Eastern Conference semifinals. Chicago would have to wait another season to get back to its winning ways.

It was worth the wait. The Bulls were almost unbeatable in 1995–96. They won an NBA record 72 games and lost only 10. The Bulls beat the Seattle SuperSonics in the Finals, four games to two. Many people consider the 1995–96 Bulls to be the best NBA team ever. *(For more on the 1995-96 Bulls, turn to page 134.)*

In 1996–97, Michael won his ninth scoring title and led the Bulls to a 69–13 record. The Bulls combined tough defense, great teamwork, and Michael's skills to win yet another championship. His Airness claimed his fifth Finals MVP trophy after the Bulls beat the Utah Jazz, four games to two.

By 1997–98, the Bulls had the second-oldest team in the NBA. But Michael was determined to win another ring. For the second season in a row, the Bulls faced the Jazz in the Finals. In Game 6, Michael poured in 45 points and nailed the series-winning jump shot with 5.2 seconds remaining!

Everyone thought that Michael's shot would be the final one of his pro career. He retired from basketball, for the second time, on January 13, 1999. But apparently Michael missed NBA action because he returned as a player with the Washington Wizards for the 2001–02 season.

The Chicago Bulls were almost unbeatable in 1995-96.

It was Michael Jordan's first full season in the NBA since his first retirement. The Bulls won an NBA record 72 games and lost only 10.

Michael averaged 30.4 points per game to win his eighth NBA scoring title. He became only the second player ever to be named MVP of the regular season, the All-Star Game, and the NBA Finals in the same season.

But the 1995-96 Bulls were not just a one-man show. Teammates Scottie Pippen, Dennis Rodman, and Toni Kukoc [KOO-coach] all played key roles. Scottie was a starter in the 1996 NBA All-Star Game. Dennis led the NBA in rebounding, with 14.9 rebounds per game. Toni was named NBA Sixth Man of the Year after averaging more than 13 points per game off the bench.

The Bulls had a record of 41–3 after the first 44 games of the 1995-96 regular season. On April 16, they beat the Milwaukee Bucks, 86–80, for their 70th win of the season. That broke the 1971-72 Los Angeles Lakers' record for most wins in a regular season.

The Bulls lost only one of their first 12 playoff games to reach the 1996 NBA Finals. They beat the Seattle SuperSonics, four games to two, in the Finals. It was a great ending to the greatest season ever.

NEW TEAMS, NEW NAMES

The NBA grew by two teams in the 1995–96 season when the Toronto Raptors and the Vancouver Grizzlies joined the league. They were the first NBA teams to be located outside the United States since 1946. Toronto and Vancouver are both in Canada.

For the 1997–98 season, the Washington Bullets changed their name to the Washington Wizards. Team owner Abe Pollin thought Washington Bullets, which had been the team's name for 23 seasons, was too violent.

1997 THEY GOT NEXT!

Women's professional basketball finally made it to the big time when the Women's National Basketball Association played its first game on June 21, 1997.

The WNBA was not the first pro league for women. But it was the first pro league that gave women a chance to show off their hoops skills and competitive drive in big arenas in major cities and on television.

Part of the league's success came from signing players who had become national stars at the 1996 Summer Olympics. Sheryl Swoopes and Rebecca Lobo signed the first WNBA player contracts on October 23, 1996. Sheryl signed with the Houston Comets and Rebecca signed with the New York Liberty. Next, Lisa Leslie signed with the Los Angeles Sparks, and Ruthie Bolton–Holifield joined the Sacramento Monarchs.

The other WNBA teams that season were the Charlotte Sting, Cleveland Rockers, Phoenix Mercury, and Utah Starzz. The Washington Mystics and Detroit Shock joined the league for the 1998 season. The Orlando Miracle and Minnesota Lynx started play in 1999. In 2000, the Indiana Fever, Miami Sol, Portland Fire, and Seattle Storm joined the league.

With Cynthia Cooper leading the way, the Houston Comets won the first four WNBA titles. They beat the New York Liberty for the championship in 1997, 1999, and 2000. In 1998, the Comets topped the Phoenix Mercury. In each playoff, Cynthia was chosen the MVP.

In 2001, Lisa Leslie led the Los Angeles Sparks to the WNBA championship over the Charlotte Sting.

FASTBREAK

Michael Jordan was at his best in big games. But for Game 5 of the 1997 NBA Finals, Michael was feeling his worst. The series between the Bulls and Utah Jazz was tied, 2–2. M.J. had a stomach flu, but he played one of the finest games of his career. He scored a game-high 38 points, including the game-winning shot. Chicago won, 90–88. Many people consider it the best game Michael ever played.

One of the most awe-inspiring parts of basketball is the perfect pass. A player is credited with an assist when his pass leads directly to a basket by a teammate. Entering the 2001-02 season, here are the eight players in NBA history with at least 7,000 career assists.

* John Stockton (14,503)

  Magic Johnson (10,141)

  Oscar Robertson (9,887)

* Mark Jackson (9,235)

  Isiah Thomas (9,061)

  Maurice Cheeks (7,392)

  Lenny Wilkens (7,211)

* Rod Strickland (7,026)   * Active

LEGEND:

CYNTHIA COOPER

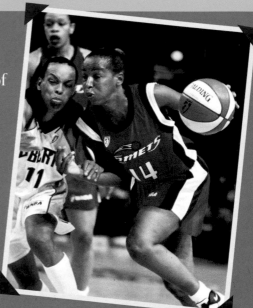

When the WNBA began play in 1997, fans expected the stars of the 1996 U.S. Summer Olympic Team to be the best players of the new league. They guessed that either Lisa Leslie of the Los Angeles Sparks, Rebecca Lobo of the New York Liberty, or Sheryl Swoopes of the Houston Comets would be the league MVP. They guessed wrong.

Houston Comet guard Cynthia Cooper turned out to be the WNBA's biggest surprise. Cynthia was 34 years old when the 1997 season began. Most fans didn't know much about her, but Cynthia could play.

Cynthia spent 11 seasons starring for pro teams in Europe. She led the European League in scoring eight times and averaged 30.5 points per game.

When Sheryl missed the first 19 games of the 1997 season to have a baby, Cynthia picked up the slack. She led the WNBA in scoring (22.2 points per game) and was named regular–season MVP. Cynthia led the Comets to the WNBA Championship, scoring 25 points against the New York Liberty in the final game.

"Not everybody gets a chance to reach their goals," Cynthia said after the 1997 season. "I've come very close to reaching every single goal that I've set for myself."

Not only was Lisa named the Playoff MVP in 2001, but she also won the league MVP and the All–Star Game MVP.

WOMEN IN STRIPES

Women made strides — and stripes — in basketball during the 1990s. Soon after the WNBA had completed its first season, women appeared in NBA games for the first time.

On October 31, 1997, Violet Palmer became the first woman to referee an official NBA game. She officiated the season opener between the Vancouver Grizzlies and the Dallas Mavericks. Five days later, female official Dee Kantner made her NBA debut.

Some male players weren't happy about having women officiate their games. But Violet and Dee did their jobs well. By the time the season ended, they had been accepted as referees, not just female referees.

THE DEAN OF BASKETBALL

Dean Smith may have been the greatest college basket-ball coach ever. He led the University of North Carolina Tar Heels to 879 wins in 36 seasons, from 1962 to 1997. No other coach has won more college games.

The Tar Heels went to 27 NCAA tournaments and 11 Final Fours under Coach Smith. They won the championship twice, in 1982 and 1993. Coach Smith, Bob Knight, and Peter Newell are the only three coaches to win an NCAA title, an NIT championship, and an Olympic gold medal.

Dean Smith coached 26 Tar Heel players who went on to become NBA first-round draft picks. The list includes Antawn Jamison, Vince Carter, Jerry Stackhouse, and Rasheed Wallace. Coach Smith's most famous player was the great Michael Jordan.

Not all of Coach Smith's players made it to the NBA, but most of them got what they went to college for: their degrees. More than 96 percent of his players graduated from North Carolina.

Coach Smith also inspired a lot of basketball careers. Over 50 of his former players went on to play pro ball in the NBA and ABA. Assistant coaches and team managers who worked under Coach Smith went on to coach at the NBA, college, or high school levels, too.

What was the secret of Coach Smith's success? It could be that he had had some good teachers along the way. Dean played for the legendary Phog Allen at the University of Kansas from 1949 to 1953. Coach Allen had been coached by Dr. James Naismith in the early 1900s. Dr. Naismith invented basketball.

THE BEST WOMEN'S COLLEGE TEAM?

How good was the University of Tennessee women's basketball team? Consider this: From 1987 to 1998, the Lady Volunteers won six championships, including three in a row in 1996, 1997, and 1998.

The 1997–98 team went 39–0 and won its games by an average of 30.1 points! No other women's team had won more than 35 games in one season.

Head coach Pat Summitt deserves much of the credit for Tennessee's success. She became the Lady Vols' coach in 1974. Through 1998, she had led the Lady Volunteers to the Final Four 15 times in 24 seasons.

On the court, Tennessee has had terrific players over the years. Perhaps the best was Chamique Holdsclaw. She played from 1995 to 1999 and became Tennessee's all–time leading scorer and rebounder. She won four New York state high school championships and three college national championships.

HIGH SCHOOL HEROES

The NBA turned 50 in 1996. But while the league was getting older, its players were getting younger.

Kevin Garnett became the first high school star to jump directly to the NBA since Bill Willoughby joined the Atlanta Hawks in 1975. Kevin was selected by the Minnesota Timberwolves with the fifth pick in the 1995 draft. Since Kevin, 18 high school draftees have declared for the draft.

Kevin wasn't the only high school star to find fame in the NBA. Kobe Bryant was selected by the Charlotte Hornets with the 13th pick of the 1996 draft. A few weeks later, Kobe was traded to the Los Angeles Lakers. Kobe wowed fans by winning the NBA Slam–Dunk Championship in his rookie season. In 1997–98, his second season, he averaged 15.4 points per game. He was selected by the fans to start in the All–Star Game. In the 1999–2000 and 2000–01 seasons, Kobe picked up NBA championships with the Lakers.

Jermaine O'Neal is another player who jumped from high school to the pros. He was chosen four picks after Kobe, by the Portland Trail Blazers. On December 5, 1996, Jermaine became the youngest person to play in an NBA game. He was only 18 years, one month, and 22 days old.

Other high school players drafted by NBA teams were Tracy McGrady (Toronto Raptors), Stephen Jackson (Phoenix Suns), Al Harrington (Indiana Pacers), Rashard Lewis (Seattle SuperSonics), and Darius Miles (Los Angeles Clippers).

2000+ THE DYNASTY OF THE NEW MILLENNIUM?

The NBA's big story at the start of the new millennium was the Los Angeles Laker's back–to–back championships in the 1999–2000 and 2000–01 seasons. The story began with the start of a new basketball era in Los Angeles at the beginning of the 1999–2000 season.

The team hired a new head coach, Phil Jackson, formerly coach of the Chicago Bulls. Coach Jackson had won six NBA titles with the Bulls. A brand–new home arena awaited Coach Jackson and his new team as the Lakers moved into the 18,997–seat STAPLES Center.

Paced by 7–foot–1 center Shaquille O'Neal and 6–foot–7 guard Kobe Bryant, the Lakers posted the best record in the league in the 1999–2000 season with a 67–15 mark. Shaq averaged a career–high 29.7 points per game while Kobe chipped in with 22.5 points per game. The Lakers won 25 of their first 30 games and had winning streaks of 16, 19, and 11 games during the regular season.

The Lakers capped off their great season with playoff series wins over the Sacramento Kings, Phoenix Suns, and Portland TrailBlazers. Then they knocked off the Indiana Pacers in the Finals, four games to two, to win their first championship since 1988. Shaq was named MVP of the Finals.

Although the Lakers faltered a bit during the 2000–01 regular season, they won the Pacific Division with a 56–26 record. In the playoffs, the Lakers posted an astonishing 11–0 record beating Portland, Sacramento, and the San Antonio Spurs in the Western Conference playoffs. The Lakers dropped Game 1 of the NBA Finals to the Philadelphia 76ers. But Los Angeles rebounded to take the next four games and the NBA championship. Shaq was once again named Finals MVP for his 33.0 points-per-game average and 15.8 rebounds-per-game average against Philadelphia.

With the nucleus of Shaq, Kobe, and Coach Jackson (winner of eight NBA titles as a coach) the Lakers are poised to become the NBA's first dynasty of the new millennium.

It's time for one last shot. Use your basketball knowledge to help answer these questions. Then you can check your score on page 147.

1 The original Dream Team earned a gold medal at the 1992 Summer Olympics. What former Duke star was the only college player on the team?

2 There were 13 NBA players with the last name Williams in 1993. Which baseball player with the same last name won a batting title for the 1998 World Champion New York Yankees?

3 Michael Jordan retired from basketball in 1993. He returned to the Bulls in March 1995. What uniform number did Michael wear for the final 17 games of the 1994-95 regular season? *(Hint: The answer is NOT number 23.)*

4 Michael Jordan, Patrick Ewing, and Chris Mullin won Olympic gold medals in 1992 and 1984. Which former Indiana University head coach was the coach of the 1984 U.S. Olympic team?

OVERTIME

ANSWERS

BASKETBALL BEGINS, 1500-1929
1 **Michael Jordan**
2 **Thomas Edison**
3 **The Dream Team**
4 **$1,230**

WHEN COLLEGE WAS KING, 1930-1945
1 **Patrick Ewing**
2 **Dennis Rodman**
3 **Kareem Abdul-Jabbar**
4 **Bill Bradley**

THE START OF THE NBA, 1946-1959
1 **Art Shell**
2 **The Los Angeles Lakers**
3 **68**
4 **Atlanta**

THE AGE OF WILT, 1960s
1 **Julius Erving**
2 **Assists**
3 **George Bush**
4 **U.S. Naval Academy**

OVERTIME

ANSWERS

BASKETBALL ROCKS AND ROLLS, 1970s

1. **Duke University**
2. **86 inches**
3. **Shaquille O'Neal**
4. **Allen Iverson**

MAGIC TIME, 1980s

1. **John Stockton**
2. **Hakeem Olajuwon**
3. **Washington, D.C.**
4. **University of Arizona**

BASKETBALL TODAY, 1990s AND 2000s

1. **Christian Laettner**
2. **Bernie Williams**
3. **Number 45**
4. **Bobby Knight**

ANSWERS

PEAK
PERFORMANCES

Since it began in 1946, the NBA has featured the greatest highflying, rim-rocking basketball players in the world. This section honors the first-rate teams and individuals in NBA history — championship winners, Rookies of the Year, MVPs, and season and single-game record holders.

>> NBA CHAMPIONS

SEASON	TEAM
2000-01	Los Angeles Lakers
1999-00	Los Angeles Lakers
1998-99	San Antonio Spurs
1997-98	Chicago Bulls
1996-97	Chicago Bulls
1995-96	Chicago Bulls
1994-95	Houston Rockets
1993-94	Houston Rockets
1992-93	Chicago Bulls
1991-92	Chicago Bulls
1990-91	Chicago Bulls
1989-90	Detroit Pistons
1988-89	Detroit Pistons
1987-88	Los Angeles Lakers
1986-87	Los Angeles Lakers
1985-86	Boston Celtics
1984-85	Los Angeles Lakers
1983-84	Boston Celtics
1982-83	Philadelphia 76ers

>> NBA
CHAMPIONS

SEASON	TEAM
1981-82	Los Angeles Lakers
1980-81	Boston Celtics
1979-80	Los Angeles Lakers
1978-79	Seattle SuperSonics
1977-78	Washington Bullets
1976-77	Portland Trail Blazers
1975-76	Boston Celtics
1974-75	Golden State Warriors
1973-74	Boston Celtics
1972-73	New York Knicks
1971-72	Los Angeles Lakers
1970-71	Milwaukee Bucks
1969-70	New York Knicks
1968-69	Boston Celtics
1967-68	Boston Celtics
1966-67	Philadelphia 76ers
1965-66	Boston Celtics
1964-65	Boston Celtics
1963-64	Boston Celtics

>> NBA CHAMPIONS

SEASON	TEAM
1962-63	Boston Celtics
1961-62	Boston Celtics
1960-61	Boston Celtics
1959-60	Boston Celtics
1958-59	Boston Celtics
1957-58	St. Louis Hawks
1956-57	Boston Celtics
1955-56	Philadelphia Warriors
1954-55	Syracuse Nationals
1953-54	Minneapolis Lakers
1952-53	Minneapolis Lakers
1951-52	Minneapolis Lakers
1950-51	Rochester Royals
1949-50	Minneapolis Lakers
1948-49	Minneapolis Lakers
1947-48	Baltimore Bullets
1946-47	Philadelphia Warriors

>> NBA ROOKIE OF THE YEAR

SEASON	PLAYER	TEAM
2000-01	Mike Miller	Orlando
1999-00	Elton Brand	Chicago
	Steve Francis	Houston
1998-99	Vince Carter	Toronto
1997-98	Tim Duncan	San Antonio
1996-97	Allen Iverson	Philadelphia
1995-96	Damon Stoudamire	Toronto
1994-95	Grant Hill	Detroit
	Jason Kidd	Dallas
1993-94	Chris Webber	Golden State
1992-93	Shaquille O'Neal	Orlando
1991-92	Larry Johnson	Charlotte
1990-91	Derrick Coleman	New Jersey
1989-90	David Robinson	San Antonio
1988-89	Mitch Richmond	Golden State
1987-88	Mark Jackson	New York
1986-87	Chuck Person	Indiana
1985-86	Patrick Ewing	New York

>> NBA ROOKIE OF THE YEAR

SEASON	PLAYER	TEAM
1984-85	Michael Jordan	Chicago
1983-84	Ralph Sampson	Houston
1982-83	Terry Cummings	San Diego
1981-82	Buck Williams	New Jersey
1980-81	Darrell Griffith	Utah
1979-80	Larry Bird	Boston
1978-79	Phil Ford	Kansas City
1977-78	Walter Davis	Phoenix
1976-77	Adrian Dantley	Buffalo
1975-76	Alvan Adams	Phoenix
1974-75	Keith Wilkes	Golden State
1973-74	Ernie DiGregorio	Buffalo
1972-73	Bob McAdoo	Buffalo
1971-72	Sidney Wicks	Portland
1970-71	Dave Cowens	Boston
	Geoff Petrie	Portland
1969-70	Kareem Abdul-Jabbar	Milwaukee

>> NBA ROOKIE OF THE YEAR

SEASON	PLAYER	TEAM
1968-69	Wes Unseld	Baltimore
1967-68	Earl Monroe	Baltimore
1966-67	Dave Bing	Detroit
1965-66	Rick Barry	San Francisco
1964-65	Willis Reed	New York
1963-64	Jerry Lucas	Cincinnati
1962-63	Terry Dischinger	Chicago
1961-62	Walt Bellamy	Chicago
1960-61	Oscar Robertson	Cincinnati
1959-60	Wilt Chamberlain	Philadelphia
1958-59	Elgin Baylor	Minneapolis
1957-58	Woody Sauldsberry	Philadelphia
1956-57	Tom Heinsohn	Boston
1955-56	Maurice Stokes	Rochester
1954-55	Bob Pettit	Milwaukee
1953-54	Ray Felix	Baltimore
1952-53	Don Meineke	Fort Wayne

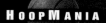

>> MOST VALUABLE PLAYER

SEASON	PLAYER	TEAM
2000-01	Allen Iverson	Philadelphia
1999-00	Shaquille O'Neal	L.A. Lakers
1998-99	Karl Malone	Utah
1997-98	Michael Jordan	Chicago
1996-97	Karl Malone	Utah
1995-96	Michael Jordan	Chicago
1994-95	David Robinson	San Antonio
1993-94	Hakeem Olajuwon	Houston
1992-93	Charles Barkley	Phoenix
1991-92	Michael Jordan	Chicago
1990-91	Michael Jordan	Chicago
1989-90	Magic Johnson	L.A. Lakers
1988-89	Magic Johnson	L.A. Lakers
1987-88	Michael Jordan	Chicago
1986-87	Magic Johnson	L.A. Lakers
1985-86	Larry Bird	Boston
1984-85	Larry Bird	Boston

>> MOST VALUABLE PLAYER

SEASON	PLAYER	TEAM
1983-84	Larry Bird	Boston
1982-83	Moses Malone	Philadelphia
1981-82	Moses Malone	Houston
1980-81	Julius Erving	Philadelphia
1979-80	Kareem Abdul-Jabbar	Los Angeles
1978-79	Moses Malone	Houston
1977-78	Bill Walton	Portland
1976-77	Kareem Abdul-Jabbar	Los Angeles
1975-76	Kareem Abdul-Jabbar	Los Angeles
1974-75	Bob McAdoo	Buffalo
1973-74	Kareem Abdul-Jabbar	Milwaukee
1972-73	Dave Cowens	Boston
1971-72	Kareem Abdul-Jabbar	Milwaukee
1970-71	Kareem Abdul-Jabbar	Milwaukee
1969-70	Willis Reed	New York
1968-69	Wes Unseld	Baltimore
1967-68	Wilt Chamberlain	Philadelphia

>> MOST VALUABLE PLAYER

SEASON	PLAYER	TEAM
1966-67	Wilt Chamberlain	Philadelphia
1965-66	Wilt Chamberlain	Philadelphia
1964-65	Bill Russell	Boston
1963-64	Oscar Robertson	Cincinnati
1962-63	Bill Russell	Boston
1961-62	Bill Russell	Boston
1960-61	Bill Russell	Boston
1959-60	Wilt Chamberlain	Philadelphia
1958-59	Bob Pettit	St. Louis
1957-58	Bill Russell	Boston
1956-57	Bob Cousy	Boston
1955-56	Bob Pettit	St. Louis

NBA'S 50 GREATEST PLAYERS

In 1996, as part of its 50th anniversary celebration, the NBA named the 50 greatest players in league history. Here are the results of a poll that included media, former players, coaches, and team executives.

PLAYER	YEARS PLAYED
Kareem Abdul-Jabbar	1969-89
Nate Archibald	1970-84
Paul Arizin	1950-62
Charles Barkley	1984-2000
Rick Barry	1965-80
Elgin Baylor	1958-72
Dave Bing	1966-78
Larry Bird	1979-92
Wilt Chamberlain	1959-73
Bob Cousy	1950-63, 1969-70
Dave Cowens	1970-80, 1982-83
Billy Cunningham	1965-76
Dave DeBusschere	1962-74
Clyde Drexler	1983-98
Julius Erving	1971-87
* Patrick Ewing	1985-

* Active

NBA'S 50 GREATEST PLAYERS

PLAYER	YEARS PLAYED
Walt Frazier	1967-80
George Gervin	1972-86
Hal Greer	1958-73
John Havlicek	1962-78
Elvin Hayes	1968-84
Magic Johnson	1979-91,1996
Sam Jones	1957-69
* Michael Jordan	1984-93, 1995-98, 2001-
Jerry Lucas	1963-74
* Karl Malone	1985-
Moses Malone	1974-95
Pete Maravich	1970-80
Kevin McHale	1980-93
George Mikan	1946-54, 55-56
Earl Monroe	1967-80
* Hakeem Olajuwon	1984-
* Shaquille O'Neal	1992-

* Active

>> NBA'S 50 GREATEST PLAYERS

PLAYER	YEARS PLAYED
Robert Parish	1976-97
Bob Pettit	1954-65
* Scottie Pippen	1987-
Willis Reed	1964-74
Oscar Robertson	1960-74
* David Robinson	1989-
Bill Russell	1956-69
Dolph Schayes	1948-64
Bill Sharman	1950-61
* John Stockton	1984-
Isiah Thomas	1981-94
Nate Thurmond	1963-77
Wes Unseld	1968-81
Bill Walton	1974-88
Jerry West	1960-74
Lenny Wilkens	1960-75
James Worthy	1982-94

* Active

>> NBA SINGLE SEASON RECORDS

SCORING AVERAGE

PLAYER	TEAM	SEASON	AVG.
Wilt Chamberlain	Philadelphia	1961-62	50.4
Wilt Chamberlain	San Francisco	1962-63	44.8
Wilt Chamberlain	Philadelphia	1960-61	38.4
Wilt Chamberlain	Philadelphia	1959-60	37.6
Michael Jordan	Chicago	1986-87	37.1
Wilt Chamberlain	San Francisco	1963-64	36.9
Rick Barry	San Francisco	1966-67	35.6
Michael Jordan	Chicago	1987-88	35.0
Elgin Baylor	Los Angeles	1960-61	34.8

FIELD-GOAL PERCENTAGE

PLAYER	TEAM	SEASON	AVG.
Wilt Chamberlain	Los Angeles	1972-73	.727
Wilt Chamberlain	San Francisco	1966-67	.683
Artis Gilmore	Chicago	1980-81	.670
Artis Gilmore	Chicago	1981-82	.652
Wilt Chamberlain	Los Angeles	1971-72	.649

NBA SINGLE SEASON RECORDS

FREE-THROW PERCENTAGE

PLAYER	TEAM	SEASON	AVG.
Calvin Murphy	Houston	1980-81	.958
Mahmoud Abdul-Rauf	Denver	1993-94	.956
Jeff Hornacek	Utah	1999-2000	.950
Mark Price	Cleveland	1992-93	.948
Mark Price	Cleveland	1991-92	.947

THREE-POINT FIELD GOAL PERCENTAGE

PLAYER	TEAM	SEASON	AVG.
Steve Kerr	Chicago	1994-95	.524
Tim Legler	Washington	1995-96	.522
Jon Sundvold	Miami	1988-89	.522
Steve Kerr	Chicago	1995-96	.515
Detlef Schrempf	Seattle	1994-95	.514

>> NBA SINGLE SEASON RECORDS

REBOUNDS

PLAYER	TEAM	SEASON	AVG.
Wilt Chamberlain	Philadelphia	1960-61	27.2
Wilt Chamberlain	Philadelphia	1959-60	27.0
Wilt Chamberlain	Philadelphia	1961-62	25.7
Bill Russell	Boston	1963-64	24.7
Wilt Chamberlain	Philadelphia	1965-66	24.6

BLOCKED SHOTS

PLAYER	TEAM	SEASON	AVG.
Mark Eaton	Utah	1984-85	5.56
Manute Bol	Washington	1985-86	4.97
Elmore Smith	Los Angeles	1973-74	4.85
Mark Eaton	Utah	1985-86	4.61
Hakeem Olajuwon	Houston	1989-90	4.59

>> NBA SINGLE SEASON RECORDS

ASSISTS

PLAYER	TEAM	SEASON	AVG.
John Stockton	Utah	1989-90	14.5
John Stockton	Utah	1990-91	14.2
Isiah Thomas	Detroit	1984-85	13.9
John Stockton	Utah	1987-88	13.8
John Stockton	Utah	1991-92	13.7
John Stockton	Utah	1988-89	13.6
Kevin Porter	Detroit	1978-79	13.4
Magic Johnson	Los Angeles	1983-84	13.1
Magic Johnson	Los Angeles	1988-89	12.8
Magic Johnson	Los Angeles	1984-85	12.6
John Stockton	Utah	1993-94	12.6

>> NBA SINGLE SEASON RECORDS

STEALS

PLAYER	TEAM	SEASON	AVG.
Alvin Robertson	San Antonio	1985-86	3.67
Don Buse	Indiana	1976-77	3.47
Magic Johnson	Los Angeles	1980-81	3.43
Micheal Richardson	New York	1979-80	3.23
Alvin Robertson	San Antonio	1986-87	3.21

>> NBA SINGLE GAME RECORDS

MOST POINTS

PLAYER	DATE	POINTS
Wilt Chamberlain	3/2/62	100
Wilt Chamberlain	12/8/61	78
Wilt Chamberlain	1/13/62	73
Wilt Chamberlain	11/16/62	73
David Thompson	4/09/78	73
Wilt Chamberlain	11/3/62	72
Elgin Baylor	11/15/60	71
David Robinson	4/24/94	71
Wilt Chamberlain	3/10/63	70
Michael Jordan	3/28/90	69
Wilt Chamberlain	12/16/67	68
Pete Maravich	2/25/77	68
Wilt Chamberlain	3/09/61	67
Wilt Chamberlain	2/17/62	67
Wilt Chamberlain	2/25/62	67
Wilt Chamberlain	1/11/63	67
Wilt Chamberlain	2/9/69	66

HOOPMANIA

>> NBA SINGLE GAME RECORDS

MOST POINTS (CONTINUED)

PLAYER	DATE	POINTS
Wilt Chamberlain	2/13/62	65
Wilt Chamberlain	2/27/62	65
Wilt Chamberlain	2/7/66	65
Elgin Baylor	11/8/59	64
Rick Barry	3/26/74	64
Michael Jordan	1/16/93	64

FIELD GOALS

PLAYER	DATE	FGS	ATTEMPTS
Wilt Chamberlain	3/2/62	36	63
Wilt Chamberlain	12/8/61	31	62
Wilt Chamberlain	12/16/67	30	40
Rick Barry	2/26/74	30	45

Wilt Chamberlain made 29 four times

>> NBA SINGLE GAME RECORDS

FREE THROWS

PLAYER	DATE	FTS	ATTEMPTS
Wilt Chamberlain	3/2/62	28	32
Adrian Dantley	1/4/84	28	29
Adrian Dantley	11/25/83	27	31
Adrian Dantley	10/31/80	26	29
Michael Jordan	2/26/87	26	27

THREE-POINT FIELD GOALS

PLAYER	DATE	FGS
Dennis Scott	4/18/96	11
Brian Shaw	4/8/93	10
Joe Dumars	11/8/94	10
George McCloud	12/16/95	10

Many tied with 9 each

>> NBA SINGLE GAME RECORDS

ASSISTS

PLAYER	DATE	ASSTS.
Scott Skiles	12/30/90	30
Kevin Porter	2/24/78	29
Bob Cousy	2/27/59	28
Guy Rodgers	3/14/63	28
John Stockton	1/15/91	28

BLOCKED SHOTS

PLAYER	DATE	BLOCKS
Elmore Smith	10/28/73	17
Manute Bol	1/25/86	15
Manute Bol	2/26/87	15
Shaquille O'Neal	11/20/93	15

>> NBA SINGLE GAME RECORDS

REBOUNDS

PLAYER	DATE	REBS
Wilt Chamberlain	11/24/60	55
Bill Russell	2/5/60	51
Bill Russell	11/16/57	49
Bill Russell	3/11/65	49
Wilt Chamberlain	2/6/60	45
Wilt Chamberlain	1/21/61	45

STEALS

PLAYER	DATE	STEALS
Larry Kenon	12/26/76	11
Kendall Gill	4/3/99	11

Fourteen different players tied with 10 each,
including Alvin Robertson, who had 10 steals
in a game four times.

>> GLOSSARY

calisthenics gymnastic exercises usually done without special equipment to develop muscular strength

commisioner an official selected by an athletic association to be in charge of a sport

dominant having the most influence or control

ejected having been thrown out

prophet a person who can foretell the future

scandal something that offends the morality of the social community

shrine a place that is considered sacred

suburb a small community close to a city

RESOURCES

BOOKS

Bayne, Bijan C. *Sky Kings: Black Pioneers of Professional Basketball.* Danbury, CT: Franklin Watts, 1997.

Boughn, Michael, Michael Goughn, and Joseph Romain. *Michael Jordan: Airborne.* Toronto, Canada: Warwick Publishing, 1999.

Corbett, Sara. *Venus to the Hoop: A Gold Medal Year in Women's Basketball.* New York, NY: Anchor Books, 1998.

Grabowski, John F. *Basketball.* Farmington Hills, MI: Lucent Books, 2001.

Gutman, Bill. *Shooting Stars: The Women of Pro Basketball.* New York, NY: Random House Children's Publishing, 1998.

Stewart, Mark. *Basketball: A History of Hoops.* Danbury, CT: Franklin Watts, 1999.

MAGAZINES

NBA Hoop and *NBA Inside Stuff*
Professional Sports Publications
355 Lexington Avenue
New York, NY 10017

>> RESOURCES

SPORTS ILLUSTRATED FOR KIDS
135 W. 50th Street
New York, NY 10020
(800) 992–0196
http://www.sikids.com

WEB SITES

SPORTS ILLUSTRATED FOR KIDS
http://www.sikids.com
Check out the latest sports news, cool games, and much more.

Visit the official Web sites of the following organizations:

National Basketball Association
http://www.nba.com

Women's National Basketball Association
http://www.wnba.com

ORGANIZATION

Naismith Memorial Basketball Hall of Fame
1150 West Colombus Avenue
Springfield, MA 01105
(413) 781–6500
http://www.hoophall.com

>> INDEX